OPPOSING VIEWPOINTS®

Religion in America

Other Books of Related Interest

OPPOSING VIEWPOINTS®

Religion in America

Mary E. Williams, *Book Editor*

Bruce Glassman, *Vice President*
Bonnie Szumski, *Publisher*
Helen Cothran, *Managing Editor*

OPPOSING
VIEWPOINTS®
SERIES

GREENHAVEN PRESS
An imprint of Thomson Gale, a part of The Thomson Corporation

THOMSON

GALE

Detroit • New York • San Francisco • San Diego • New Haven, Conn.
Waterville, Maine • London • Munich

THOMSON
————✳————™
GALE

For more information, contact
Greenhaven Press
27500 Drake Rd.
Farmington Hills, MI 48331-3535
Or you can visit our Internet site at http://www.gale.com

LIBRARY OF CONGRESS CATALOGING-IN-PUBLICATION DATA
Religion in America / Mary E. Williams, book editor. 　　p. cm. — (Opposing viewpoints series) 　Includes bibliographical references and index. 　ISBN 0-7377-2957-0 (lib. : alk. paper) — ISBN 0-7377-2958-9 (pbk. : alk. paper) 　　1. Religion and politics—United States. 2. United States—Religion. I. Williams, Mary E., 1960– . II. Opposing viewpoints series (Unnumbered) 　BL2525.R4645 2006 　200'.973—dc22   2005040386

Printed in the United States of America

"Congress shall make no law...abridging the freedom of speech, or of the press."

First Amendment to the U.S. Constitution

The basic foundation of our democracy is the First Amendment guarantee of freedom of expression. The Opposing Viewpoints Series is dedicated to the concept of this basic freedom and the idea that it is more important to practice it than to enshrine it.

Contents

Why Consider Opposing Viewpoints?

"The only way in which a human being can make some approach to knowing the whole of a subject is by hearing what can be said about it by persons of every variety of opinion and studying all modes in which it can be looked at by every character of mind. No wise man ever acquired his wisdom in any mode but this."

John Stuart Mill

In our media-intensive culture it is not difficult to find differing opinions. Thousands of newspapers and magazines and dozens of radio and television talk shows resound with differing points of view. The difficulty lies in deciding which opinion to agree with and which "experts" seem the most credible. The more inundated we become with differing opinions and claims, the more essential it is to hone critical reading and thinking skills to evaluate these ideas. Opposing Viewpoints books address this problem directly by presenting stimulating debates that can be used to enhance and teach these skills. The varied opinions contained in each book examine many different aspects of a single issue. While examining these conveniently edited opposing views, readers can develop critical thinking skills such as the ability to compare and contrast authors' credibility, facts, argumentation styles, use of persuasive techniques, and other stylistic tools. In short, the Opposing Viewpoints Series is an ideal way to attain the higher-level thinking and reading skills so essential in a culture of diverse and contradictory opinions.

In addition to providing a tool for critical thinking, Opposing Viewpoints books challenge readers to question their own strongly held opinions and assumptions. Most people form their opinions on the basis of upbringing, peer pressure, and personal, cultural, or professional bias. By reading carefully balanced opposing views, readers must directly confront new ideas as well as the opinions of those with whom they disagree. This is not to simplistically argue that everyone who reads opposing views will—or should—change his or her opinion. Instead, the series enhances readers' understanding of their own views by encouraging confrontation with opposing ideas. Careful examination of others' views can lead to the readers' understanding of the logical inconsistencies in their own opinions, perspective on why they hold an opinion, and the consideration of the possibility that their opinion requires further evaluation.

Evaluating Other Opinions

To ensure that this type of examination occurs, Opposing Viewpoints books present all types of opinions. Prominent spokespeople on different sides of each issue as well as well-known professionals from many disciplines challenge the reader. An additional goal of the series is to provide a forum for other, less known, or even unpopular viewpoints. The opinion of an ordinary person who has had to make the decision to cut off life support from a terminally ill relative, for example, may be just as valuable and provide just as much insight as a medical ethicist's professional opinion. The editors have two additional purposes in including these less known views. One, the editors encourage readers to respect others' opinions—even when not enhanced by professional credibility. It is only by reading or listening to and objectively evaluating others' ideas that one can determine whether they are worthy of consideration. Two, the inclusion of such viewpoints encourages the important critical thinking skill of objectively evaluating an author's credentials and bias. This evaluation will illuminate an author's reasons for taking a particular stance on an issue and will aid in readers' evaluation of the author's ideas.

It is our hope that these books will give readers a deeper understanding of the issues debated and an appreciation of the complexity of even seemingly simple issues when good and honest people disagree. This awareness is particularly important in a democratic society such as ours in which people enter into public debate to determine the common good. Those with whom one disagrees should not be regarded as enemies but rather as people whose views deserve careful examination and may shed light on one's own.

Thomas Jefferson once said that "difference of opinion leads to inquiry, and inquiry to truth." Jefferson, a broadly educated man, argued that "if a nation expects to be ignorant and free . . . it expects what never was and never will be." As individuals and as a nation, it is imperative that we consider the opinions of others and examine them with skill and discernment. The Opposing Viewpoints Series is intended to help readers achieve this goal.

David L. Bender and Bruno Leone,
Founders

Greenhaven Press anthologies primarily consist of previously published material taken from a variety of sources, including periodicals, books, scholarly journals, newspapers, government documents, and position papers from private and public organizations. These original sources are often edited for length and to ensure their accessibility for a young adult audience. The anthology editors also change the original titles of these works in order to clearly present the main thesis of each viewpoint and to explicitly indicate the opinion presented in the viewpoint. These alterations are made in consideration of both the reading and comprehension levels of a young adult audience. Every effort is made to ensure that Greenhaven Press accurately reflects the original intent of the authors included in this anthology.

Introduction

"It's time to spark a real debate in this country over what the most important 'religious issues' and 'moral values' in politics are—and how broadly and deeply they are understood."

—*Jim Wallis*

In a widely publicized 1999 statement, conservative activist Paul Weyrich claimed that American society was becoming an "ever-wider sewer" and that the United States was "caught up in a cultural collapse of historic proportions." Taking note of continuing controversies such as abortion, "antireligious entertainment," and the personal immorality of political leaders, Weyrich argued that social conservatives had failed to implement a political agenda that would protect the country's traditional religious values: "A moral majority no longer exists in America. We [conservatives] probably have lost the overall culture war." Weyrich advised conservatives to "drop out" of American cultural and political life and develop new institutions to preserve Judeo-Christian civilization as the surrounding culture fell into ruin.

Just five years later, in 2004, many observers declared that the tables had turned. Exit polls taken on the day of that year's particularly contentious presidential election asked voters to name the most important issue that influenced their vote. Twenty-two percent chose "moral values," edging out two other hotly debated issues—terrorism and the economy—as the deciding factor of the election. Moreover, the majority of those who stated that moral values had the greatest effect on their decision voted for George W. Bush, the Republican incumbent who had championed bans on homosexual marriage and increased restrictions on abortion. Many social and religious conservatives—especially evangelical Christians—saw Bush's reelection as a victory for traditional family values and as a mandate to pursue faith-based agendas in the political arena.

The rallying cry for most of these religious "values voters," commentators argued, was same-sex marriage—an issue that turned up as a ballot measure in several states during the 2004 election. As Roberta Combs, president of the evangelical-based Christian Coalition, stated after the election, "We are pleased that both the executive branch and the legislative branch will be controlled by pro-family conservatives and that every one of the 11 state constitutional amendments to ban homosexual 'marriages' passed overwhelmingly. There is no doubt that because [of the legalization of same-sex marriage in Massachusetts in 2003], there was a conservative backlash which played a major role in the election outcome. . . . Christian evangelicals made the major difference."

In the weeks following the election, however, many analysts questioned the exit polls and challenged the often-stated conclusion that the so-called values voters were expressing the will of the majority of Americans of faith. For one thing, the exit polls had assumed that the phrase "moral values" was representative of the traditionalist view concerning marriage and abortion but not the moderate or liberal positions on the economy, health care, or the war in Iraq. This discrepancy was revealed in a postelection poll conducted by Zogby International. According to this poll, when asked "which moral issue most influenced your vote," 42 percent chose the war in Iraq while 13 percent picked abortion and 9 percent said same-sex marriage. When asked to define the most urgent moral problem in America, 33 percent selected "greed and materialism," 31 percent picked "poverty and economic injustice," 16 percent said abortion, and 12 percent chose same-sex marriage. The Zogby survey suggests that the exit polls had ignored the fact that issues like health care and consumerism might be defined as moral or religious issues.

Thus, while many commentators see the 2004 election results as evidence of a "cultural divide" between religious (allegedly conservative) and secular (allegedly liberal) Americans, the Zogby poll implies that the situation is more complex. For one thing, those who describe themselves as religious do not always fall neatly into "conservative" or "liberal" categories. Various surveys show, for instance, that a substantial majority of religiously observant Americans agree that the disadvantaged need government assistance to help them succeed—a viewpoint that is typically labeled as "liberal." Most also favor antipoverty programs, even if they increase taxes, as well as stricter environmental regulations—ideas also usually described as liberal. Furthermore, traditionalist evangelicals, generally portrayed as being strong opponents of abortion, often take a more moderate stance on this issue, with 52 percent stating that the procedure should be legal in some circumstances.

In the opinion of Protestant minister Jim Wallis, the cultural divide is largely a split between vocal minorities of religious and secular activists that has begun to reverberate among the public at large. "While some Democrats are now realizing the importance of faith, values, and cultural issues, a strong group of 'secular fundamentalists' still fights to keep moral and spiritual language out of the liberal discussion," Wallis maintains. "And while some Republicans would like to see an expanded application of faith, the 'religious fundamentalists' still want to restrict religious values to gay marriage and abortion." What the nation really needs, Wallis concludes, is a deeper discussion about which moral issues are of concern to a broader spectrum of ordinary religious and secular Americans.

The place of religion in America's cultural and political realm is one of many contentious issues examined in *Opposing Viewpoints: Religion in America*. Contributors provide diverse views on both the private religious attitudes of Americans and the social significance of religious belief in the following chapters: Is America a Religious Nation? What Effect Does Religion Have on American Society? What Should Be Done to Accommodate Religious Freedom in America? What Values Should Religious Americans Support? This sampling of contemporary debates illustrates how religion can be both a divisive and unifying force in American society.

CHAPTER 1

Is America a Religious Nation?

Chapter Preface

Several major polls suggest that the United States is a religious nation. According to Gallup surveys, for example, 95 percent of Americans believe in God—a number that has remained consistent over several decades and that is significantly higher than in many other industrialized nations. (In comparison, 76 percent of people in Britain and 52 percent of people in Sweden profess belief in God.) Furthermore, 65 percent of American poll respondents belong to a church or synagogue, between 57 and 65 percent agree that religion is very important in their lives, and 60 percent claim that they pray daily. Such statistics lead many observers to conclude that the American worldview comprises a unique combination of reason, democratic values, and deep religious faith. As religion scholar Michael Novak maintains, "One thing being American means is believing, more than people from most other nations do, that there should be a close relation between reason and faith."

Upon closer examination, however, the above statistics may be less revealing than they first seem. Those who list themselves as members of a church may attend church irregularly or rarely. Even those who attend church regularly may do so for nonreligious reasons—to socialize, to spend time with family members, or to conform to community expectations. In addition, people who claim that they are "believers" often differ on how they define God. Some embrace traditional definitions and see God as an all-knowing divine creator who rules the universe; others have adopted less traditional religious views, conceiving of God as a pervasive spirit, a life force, or a state of human consciousness. Thus, even people who claim to believe have widely varying views on how important religion is in their lives. Such differences of opinion may partly explain the results of the 2001 American Religious Identification Survey, which revealed that 14 percent of the nation—roughly 29.4 million Americans— have no religious affiliation. Because an earlier 1990 survey reported that 7.5 percent of Americans belonged to no religion, some scholars have drawn the conclusion that the number of "nonreligious" Americans doubled in just eleven years. As reporter Julia Duin points out, "The 2001 survey found a wide and possibly growing swath of secularism in the American population that scholars and politicians frequently ignore."

Yet it is also difficult to determine whether the growing numbers of those who hold no official religious affiliation indicate an increase in secularism in America. While some of the 14 percent of so-called nonreligious Americans are undoubtedly atheists or agnostics, some of them are also believers who have become disenchanted with institutionalized religion. Nonchurchgoers cite several reasons for skipping church, including the hypocrisy of organized religions, the inflexible beliefs of adherents, and noncompelling messages from religious leaders. Andy Butcher, a writer for *Charisma*, a magazine that chronicles trends in Pentecostal churches, reports finding "in a series of interviews with average nonchurchgoers across the country that a great many who consider themselves to be spiritual or religious have little or no time for church or the people who go there."

As the above examples illustrate, it is difficult to arrive at a single conclusion on what role religion plays in American life. The authors in the following chapter provide additional opinions on different aspects of this question.

*"[The] men who led America into
revolution and independence never doubted
for an instant that America is a 'nation
under God.'"*

America Was Founded on Religious Principles

Jeff Jacoby

In the following viewpoint Jeff Jacoby argues that religious belief is an essential element of American nationhood. America's founders believed that they were acting in accordance with divine will as they launched the struggle for independence from England. Moreover, Jacoby contends, America's early leaders recognized that religion and morality were necessary to the maintenance of liberty and good government. Jacoby is a columnist for the *Boston Globe*.

As you read, consider the following questions:

1. What reference to God is found in the Constitution, according to Jacoby?
2. According to the author, what did John Adams believe to be the purpose of the settlement of America?
3. What were Thomas Jefferson's views on religion and politics in America, according to Jacoby?

Jeff Jacoby, "God Wasn't Optional to the Founders," *Boston Globe*, July 4, 2002.
Copyright © 2002 by Globe Newspaper Company. Reproduced by permission.

M ichael Newdow, the atheist who went to court to get the Pledge of Allegiance declared unconstitutional, spent his 15 minutes of fame [in the summer of 2002] asserting that the Founding Fathers would have cheered his campaign against the words "under God."

"He is confident," the *Washington Post* reported, "that the framers of the Constitution would have supported his view, noting that they did not mention God in the nation's founding document." He had earlier made the same claim on television, telling Katie Couric, "There is no reference to God in the Constitution. It's striking . . . that it is missing."

God in the Constitution

As it happens, there *is* a reference to God in the Constitution, a specifically Christian reference: "Done in Convention by the Unanimous consent of the States present," the final sentence begins, "the Seventeenth Day of September in the *Year of our Lord* one thousand seven hundred and Eighty seven. . . ." If the Framers were as determined as Newdow seems to think they were that the political system they were crafting be sanitized of any hint of God, surely they would have found a different way to date their document.

In fact, the last thing the founders of the American republic wanted was a public square from which every reference to God was removed. "Americans of the founding generation appealed without flinching to the undeceivable Judge of all consciences," Michael Novak writes in *On Two Wings*, his stirring . . . book on the centrality of religion to American nationhood, "precisely because they believed they had formed a covenant with Him, in the name of His most precious gift to the universe, the liberty of the sons of God."

Trying to make sense of the creation of the United States with reference only to its Enlightenment underpinnings is, in Novak's metaphor, "to cut off one of the two wings by which the American eagle flies." The philosophy of liberty developed by thinkers such as John Locke and Charles Montesquieu was crucial in shaping the ideas later embodied in the Declaration of Independence and Constitution, but it was only half the story. Religion was the other half.

The Pledge of Allegiance wasn't written until late in the

19th century; the phrase "under God" wasn't added until halfway through the 20th. But the 18th-century men who led America into revolution and independence never doubted for an instant that America is a "nation under God."

A Profession of Faith

In his first official act, Pres. George Washington did something that would be unthinkable today: He prayed in public! Specifically, during his inaugural address, he made "fervent supplications to that Almighty Being who rules over the universe, who presides in the councils of nations, and whose providential aids can supply every human defect, that His benediction may consecrate to the liberties and happiness of the people of the United States a Government instituted by themselves for these essential purposes. . . . No people can be bound to acknowledge and adore the Invisible Hand which conducts the affairs of men more than the people of the United States. Every step by which they have advanced to the character of an independent nation seems to have been distinguished by some token of providential agency."

If that were not enough, Washington added: "We ought to be no less persuaded that the propitious smiles of Heaven can never be expected on a nation that disregards the eternal rules of order and right which Heaven itself has ordained."

Roy S. Moore, *USA Today Magazine*, September 2000.

For freedom, they believed, was what God intended for His human creatures—the freedom to be faithful to God's purposes and to follow the course He had set out in the Bible. In fighting for liberty and in establishing a republic, they were advancing God's vision for mankind; they saw their young nation as a new Israel, a people chosen by the Almighty and liberated with His help so they might build a society worthy of His ideals.

"I always consider the settlement of America with reverence and wonder," John Adams wrote in 1765, "as the opening of a grand scene and design in Providence for the illumination of the ignorant and the emancipation of the slavish part of mankind all over the earth."

It was a point others would make again and again, both in the years leading up to the war with England, and long after that war was won.

In an influential sermon in 1776, the Rev. John Wither-spoon—James Madison's teacher at Princeton and a leading member of the Continental Congress—argued that God's hand could be discerned in the gathering storm and in the chain of events that had led to it. "It would be a criminal inat-tention," he said, "not to observe the singular interposition of Providence hitherto, in behalf of the American colonies."

At a very different moment 11 years later, reflecting on the remarkable unanimity achieved by the Constitutional Convention—a body that should have been riven by bicker-ing factions—Madison likewise saw divine intervention.

"It is impossible," he wrote in Federalist No. 37, "for the man of pious reflection not to perceive in it a finger of the Almighty hand which has been so frequently and signally ex-tended to our relief in the critical stages of the revolution."

Religious Conviction Is Not Optional

But a nation under God is not just a nation whose destiny has been guided by Heaven. It is a nation, the Founders in-sisted, that never forgets that there is, as the Declaration put it, a "Supreme Judge of the World" who holds men and women responsible for their deeds. To them, awareness of God was not optional—not if American liberty and republi-can government were to succeed.

"Of all the dispositions and habits which lead to political prosperity, religion and morality are *indispensable* supports," George Washington avowed in his Farewell Address. It was a conviction he shared with most of his contemporaries.

Indeed, the idea that government support for religion is incompatible with the First Amendment would have struck the Framers of that amendment as ludicrous. On the same day the First Congress approved the constitutional language prohibiting "an establishment of religion," it also passed the Northwest Ordinance, which authorized a government for the territory north of the Ohio River. "Religion, morality, and knowledge, being necessary to good government and the happiness of mankind," the law specified, "schools and the means of education shall forever be encouraged."

Even Thomas Jefferson, though skeptical of much that he read in the Bible, believed that inculcating Judeo-Christian virtue was essential for America's political well-being. For that reason, he not only made a point of attending church, but used federal funds to support the weekly religious services held in the capitol and other government buildings.

Much has changed in the last [two centuries], but the health of our political institutions still depends on our ethics and religion. The men of 1776 have long since gone to their reward, but it remains our responsibility to preserve today what they envisioned so long ago: one nation under God, with liberty and justice for all.

"[The Founders'] own statements—not dead rhetoric but alive with ringing, still radical, ideas—can reconnect us to our proud, secular roots."

America Was Founded on Secular Principles

Robin Morgan

Contemporary politicians often claim that America was founded on religious principles. Robin Morgan challenges this notion in the following viewpoint, arguing that the founders themselves often criticized religion and embraced secular ideals, which reject the mixing of religion and government. George Washington and John Adams, for example, signed a treaty proclaiming that the United States was not "founded on the Christian Religion." Other early American leaders, such as Thomas Jefferson, questioned the existence of God and argued against the establishment of a Christian theocracy, Morgan points out. Morgan is an emeritus editor of *Ms.* magazine and the author of several books on feminism, culture, and politics.

As you read, consider the following questions:
1. In Morgan's opinion, what do the terms *Nature's God* and *Creator*, which are included in the Declaration of Independence, actually refer to?
2. What were Thomas Paine's views on religion, according to the author?
3. In what way did George Washington express his disbelief in Christianity, according to Morgan?

Robin Morgan, "Ashcroft and Friends vs. Washington and the Framers: Fighting Words for a Secular America," *Ms. Magazine*, vol. 14, Fall 2004, pp. 47–49.

Americans who honor the U.S. Constitution's strict separation of church and state are now genuinely alarmed. Agnostics and atheists, as well as observant people of every faith, fear—sensibly—that the religious right is gaining historic political power, via an ultraconservative movement with highly placed friends. But many of us feel helpless. We haven't read the Founding Documents since school (if then). We lack arguing tools, "verbal karate" evidence we can cite in defending a secular United States.

For instance, such extremists claim—and, too often, we ourselves assume—that U.S. law has religious roots. Yet the Constitution contains no reference to a deity. The Declaration of Independence contains not one word on religion, basing its authority on the shocking idea that power is derived from ordinary people, which challenged European traditions of rule by divine right and/or heavenly authority. (Remember, George III was king of England *and* anointed head of its church.) The words "Nature's God," the "Creator" and "divine Providence" do appear in the Declaration. But in its contexts—an era, and author, Thomas Jefferson, that celebrated science and the Enlightenment—these words are analogous to our contemporary phrase "life force."

Not Founded on the Christian Religion

[Christian fundamentalist] Jerry Falwell notoriously blamed [the terrorist attacks of September 11, 2001] on "pagans, abortionists, feminists, gays and lesbians . . . [and other groups] who have tried to secularize America." He's a bit late: In 1798, Alexander Hamilton accused Jefferson of a "conspiracy to establish atheism on the ruins of Christianity" in the new republic.

Deputy Undersecretary of Defense for Intelligence William Boykin thunders, "We're a Christian nation." But the 1796 Treaty of Tripoli—initiated by George Washington and signed into law by John Adams—proclaims: "*The Government of the United States of America is not, in any sense, founded on the Christian Religion.*"

Offices for "Faith-Based Initiatives" with nearly $20 billion in grants have been established (by executive order, circumventing Congress) in 10 federal agencies, as well as *inside* the White House. This fails "the Lemon Test," violating a 1971 Supreme Court decision (*Lemon v. Kurtzman*): "first, a statute [or public policy] must have a secular legislative purpose; second, its principal or primary effect must be one that neither advances nor inhibits religion; finally, the statute [or policy] must not foster 'excessive government entanglement with religion.'"

Who Were the Founders?

When [former] Attorney General John Ashcroft repeatedly invokes religion, the Founders must be picketing in their graves. They were a mix of freethinkers, atheists, Christians, agnostics, Freemasons and Deists (professing belief in powers scientifically evinced in the natural universe). They surely were imperfect. Some were slaveholders. Female citizens were invisible to them—though Abigail Adams warned her husband John, "If particular care and attention is not paid to the Ladies, we are determined to foment a Rebellion, and will not hold ourselves bound by any Laws in which we have no voice, or Representation."

Separating Church and State

The first colony of English-speaking Europeans was Jamestown, settled in 1609 for trade, not for religious freedom. Fewer than half of the 102 Mayflower passengers in 1620 were "Pilgrims" seeking religious freedom. The secular United States of America was formed more than a century and a half later. If tradition required us to return to the views of a few early settlers, why not adopt the polytheistic and natural beliefs of the Native Americans, the true founders of the continent at least 12,000 years earlier?

Most of the religious colonial governments excluded and persecuted those of the "wrong" faith. The framers of our Constitution in 1787 wanted no part of religious intolerance and bloodshed, wisely establishing the first government in history to separate church and state.

Dan Barker, Freedom from Religion Foundation, no date.

But the Founders were, after all, *revolutionaries*. Their passion—especially regarding secularism—glows in the documents they forged and in their personal words.

Thomas Paine

Paine's writings heavily influenced the other Founders. A freethinker who opposed all organized religion, he reserved particular vituperation for Christianity.

"My country is the world and my religion is to do good" (*The Rights of Man*, 1791).

"I do not believe in the creed professed by the Jewish church, by the Roman church, by the Greek church, by the Turkish church, by the Protestant church, nor by any church that I know of. My own mind is my own church" (*The Age of Reason*, 1794).

"Of all the systems of religion that ever were invented, there is no more derogatory to the Almighty, more unedifying to man, more repugnant to reason, and more contradictory in itself than this thing called Christianity" (Ibid.).

Benjamin Franklin

Raised a Calvinist, Franklin rebelled—and spread that rebellion, affecting Adams and Jefferson. His friend, Dr. Priestley, wrote in his own *Autobiography:* It is much to be lamented that a man of Franklin's general good character and great influence should have been an unbeliever in Christianity, and also have done as much as he did to make others unbelievers. A scientist, Franklin rejected churches, rituals, and all "supernatural superstitions."

"Scarcely was I arrived at fifteen years of age, when, after having doubted in turn of different tenets, according as I found them combated in the different books that I read, I began to doubt of Revelation itself" (Franklin's *Autobiography*, 1817–18).

"Some volumes against Deism fell into my hands . . . they produced an effect precisely the reverse to what was intended by the writers; for the arguments of the Deists, which were cited in order to be refuted, appeared to me much more forcibly than the refutation itself; in a word, I soon became a thorough Deist" (Ibid.).

George Washington

The false image of Washington as a devout Christian was fabricated by Mason Locke Weems, a clergyman who also invented the cherry-tree fable and in 1800 published his *Life of George Washington*. Washington, a Deist and a Freemason, never once mentioned the name of Jesus Christ in any of his thousands of letters, and pointedly referred to divinity as "It." Whenever he (rarely) attended church, Washington always deliberately left before communion, demonstrating disbelief in Christianity's central ceremony.

John Adams

Adams, a Unitarian inspired by the Enlightenment, fiercely opposed doctrines of supernaturalism or damnation, writing to Jefferson: "I almost shudder at the thought of alluding to the most fatal example of the abuses of grief which the history of mankind has preserved—the Cross. Consider what calamities that engine of grief has produced!"

Adams realized how politically crucial—and imperiled—a secular state would be:

"The United States of America have exhibited, perhaps, the first example of governments erected on the simple principles of nature; and if men are now sufficiently enlightened to disabuse themselves of artifice, imposture, hypocrisy, and superstition, they will consider this event as an era in their history. . . . It will never be pretended that any persons employed in that service [forming the U.S. government] had interviews with the gods, or were in any degree under the influence of Heaven, more than those at work upon ships or houses, or laboring in merchandise or agriculture; it will forever be acknowledged that these governments were contrived merely by the use of reason and the senses. . . . Thirteen governments [of the original states] thus founded on the natural authority of the people alone, without a pretence of miracle or mystery . . . are a great point gained in favor of the rights of mankind" (*A Defence of the Constitutions of Government of the United States of America*, 1787–88).

Thomas Jefferson

It's a commonly stated error that U.S. law, based on English common law, is thus grounded in Judeo-Christian tradition. Yet Jefferson (writing to Dr. Thomas Cooper, February 10, 1814) noted that common law "is that system of law which was introduced by the Saxons on their settlement in England . . . about the middle of the fifth century. But Christianity was not introduced till the seventh century. . . . *We may safely affirm (though contradicted by all the judges and writers on earth) that Christianity neither is, nor ever was a part of the common law.*"

Jefferson professed disbelief in the Trinity and the divinity of Jesus Christ, while respecting moral teachings by whomever might have been a historical Jesus. He cut up a Bible, assembling his own version: "The whole history of these books [the Gospels] is so defective and doubtful," he wrote Adams (January 24, 1814), "evidence that parts have proceeded from an extraordinary man; and that other parts are of the fabric of very inferior minds."

Scorning miracles, saints, salvation, damnation, and angelic presences, Jefferson embraced reason, materialism, and science. He challenged Patrick Henry, who wanted a Christian theocracy:

"[A]n amendment was proposed by inserting 'Jesus Christ,' so that [the preamble] should read 'A departure from the plan of Jesus Christ, the holy author of our religion'; the insertion was rejected by a great majority, in proof that they meant to comprehend, within the mantle of its protection, the Jew and the Gentile, the Christian and Mohammedan, the Hindoo and Infidel of every denomination" (from Jefferson's *Autobiography*, referring to the Statute of Virginia for Religious Freedom).

The theme is consistent throughout Jefferson's prolific correspondence:

"Question with boldness even the existence of a God" (letter to Peter Carr, August 10, 1787).

"[The clergy] believe that any portion of power confided to me, will be exerted in opposition to their schemes. And they believe rightly: for I have sworn upon the altar of God, eternal hostility against every form of tyranny over the mind of man" (letter to Dr. Benjamin Rush, September 23, 1800).

"I contemplate with sovereign reverence that act of the whole American people which . . . thus [built] a wall of separation between church and state" (letter to the Danbury [Connecticut] Baptist Association, January 1, 1802).

"History, I believe, furnishes no example of a priest-ridden people maintaining a free civil government" (letter to Alexander von Humboldt, December 6, 1813).

"In every country and in every age, the priest has been hostile to liberty. He is always in alliance with the despot, abetting his abuses in return for protection to his own" (letter to Horatio G. Spafford, March 17, 1814).

"[W]hence arises the morality of the Atheist? . . . Their virtue, then, must have had some other foundation than the love of God" (letter to Thomas Law, June 13, 1814).

"I am of a sect by myself, as far as I know" (letter to Ezra Stiles, June 25, 1819).

"The day will come when the mystical generation of Jesus . . . will be classed with the fable of the generation of Minerva in the brain of Jupiter" (letter to John Adams, April 11, 1823).

James Madison

Although prayer groups proliferate in today's Congress, James Madison, "father of the Constitution," denounced even the presence of *chaplains* in Congress—*and* in the armed forces— as unconstitutional. He opposed all use of "religion as an engine of civil policy," and accurately prophesied the threat of "ecclesiastical corporations."

"Religious bondage shackles and debilitates the mind and unfits it for every noble enterprise" (letter to William Bradford, April 1, 1774).

"During almost fifteen centuries has the legal establishment of Christianity been on trial. What have been its fruits? More or less in all places, pride and indolence in the Clergy, ignorance and servility in the laity; in both, superstition, bigotry and persecution" (*Memorial and Remonstrance Against Religious Assessments*, Section 7, 1785).

"What influence in fact have ecclesiastical establishments had on Civil Society? In some instances they have been seen to erect a spiritual tyranny on the ruins of the Civil authority; in many instances they have been seen upholding the thrones of political tyranny: in no instance have they been seen as the guardians of the liberties of the people. Rulers who wished to subvert the public liberty, may have found an established Clergy convenient auxiliaries" (Ibid., Section 8).

"Besides the danger of a direct mixture of Religion & civil Government, there is an evil which ought to be guarded agst. in the indefinite accumulation of property from the capacity of holding it in perpetuity by ecclesiastical corporations. The power of all corporations ought to be limited in this respect. . . . The establishment of the chaplainship to Congs. is a palpable violation of equal rights, as well as of Constitutional principles. . . . Better also to disarm in the same way, the precedent of Chaplainships for the army and navy. . . . Religious proclamations by the Executive [branch] recommending thanksgivings & fasts are shoots from the same root. . . . Altho' recommendations only, they imply a religious agency, making no part of the trust delegated to political rulers" (*Monopolies, Perpetuities, Corporations, Ecclesiastical Endowments*, circa 1819).

That's only a sampling, quotes that blast cobwebs off the tamed images we have of the Founders. Their own statements—not dead rhetoric but alive with ringing, still radical, ideas—can reconnect us to our proud, secular roots, and should inspire us to honor and defend them. The Founders minced no words—and they acted on them.

Dare we do less?

"Americans . . . are quite possibly more committed . . . to their Christian identity than at any time in their history."

Americans Are Committed to Their Christian Identity

Samuel Huntington

Americans have always been overwhelmingly religious and Christian, argues Samuel Huntington in the following viewpoint. Early settlers founded new communities in America largely for religious reasons, and the United States was established by those who held or who respected the religious mind-set, the author points out. The separation of church and state—often cited as evidence for American secularism— was actually established to ensure the freedom and protection of religion, states Huntington. Moreover, he concludes, Americans today still affirm their Christian identity and actively practice their faith while tolerating the presence of minority religions. Huntington is a political science professor and chair of the Harvard Academy of International and Area Studies. This viewpoint is adapted from his book *Who Are We? The Challenges to America's National Identity.*

As you read, consider the following questions:

1. What percentage of Americans identify themselves as Christian, according to Huntington?
2. In Huntington's opinion, what effect has an increase in non-Christian believers had on America's religious identity?

Samuel Huntington, "Are We a Nation 'Under God?'" *The American Enterprise*, vol. 15, July/August 2004, pp. 18–23, 39. Copyright © 2004 by the American Enterprise Institute for Public Policy Research. Reproduced by permission of *The American Enterprise*, a magazine of Politics, Business, and Culture. On the Web at www.TAEmag.com.

In June [2004], the U.S. Supreme Court is considering whether the words "under God" in the Pledge of Allegiance are a violation of the separation of church and state. In 2002, a three-judge panel of the Ninth Circuit Court of Appeals in San Francisco decided by a two-to-one vote that the phrase represented an un-Constitutional "endorsement of religion" and "a profession of religious belief . . . in monotheism."

President [George W.] Bush termed this decision "ridiculous." [Then]–Senate minority leader Tom Daschle (D-SD) called it "nuts"; Governor George Pataki of New York said it was "junk justice." The Senate passed a resolution, 99 to zero, urging that the decision be reversed, and members of the House of Representatives gathered on the steps of the Capitol to recite the Pledge and sing "God Bless America." A *Newsweek* poll found that 87 percent of the public supported inclusion of the words, while 9 percent were opposed. Eighty-four percent also said they approved of references to God in public settings, including schools and government buildings, so long as no "specific religion" was mentioned.

America's Religious Identity

This battle over the Pledge has stimulated vigorous controversy on an issue central to America's identity. Opponents of "under God" (which was added to the pledge in 1954) argue that the United States is a secular country, that the First Amendment prohibits rhetorical or material state support for religion, and that people should be able to pledge allegiance to their country without implicitly also affirming a belief in God. Supporters point out that the phrase is perfectly consonant with the views of the framers of the Constitution, that Lincoln had used these words in the Gettysburg Address, and that the Supreme Court has long held that no one could be compelled to say the Pledge.

The man who brought this court challenge, Michael Newdow, aims "to ferret out all insidious uses of religion in daily life," according to the *New York Times*. "Why should I be made to feel like an outsider?" he asked. The Court of Appeals in San Francisco agreed that the words "under God" sent "a message to unbelievers that they are outsiders, not full members of the political community."

Newdow and the court majority got it right: Atheists are "outsiders" in the American community. Americans are one of the most religious people in the world, particularly compared to the peoples of other highly industrialized democracies. But they nonetheless tolerate and respect the rights of atheists and nonbelievers. Unbelievers do not have to recite the Pledge, or engage in any religiously tainted practice of which they disapprove. They also, however, do not have the right to impose their atheism on all those Americans whose beliefs now and historically have defined America as a religious nation.

A Christian Nation

Statistics say America is not only a religious nation but also a Christian one. Up to 85 percent of Americans identify themselves as Christians. Brian Cronin, who litigated against a cross on public land in Boise, Idaho, complained, "For Buddhists, Jews, Muslims, and other non-Christians in Boise, the cross only drives home the point that they are strangers in a strange land." Like Newdow and the Ninth Circuit judges, Cronin was on target. America is a predominantly Christian nation with a secular government. Non-Christians may legitimately see themselves as strangers because they or their ancestors moved to this "strange land" founded and peopled by Christians—even as Christians become strangers by moving to Israel, India, Thailand, or Morocco.

Americans have been extremely religious and overwhelmingly Christian throughout their history. The seventeenth century settlers founded their communities in America in large part for religious reasons. Eighteenth century Americans and their leaders saw their Revolution in religious and largely biblical terms. The Revolution reflected their "covenant with God" and was a war between "God's elect" and the British "Antichrist." Jefferson, Paine, and other Deists and nonbelievers felt it necessary to invoke religion to justify the Revolution. The Continental Congress declared days of fasting to implore the forgiveness and help of God, and days of thanksgiving for what He had done to promote their cause. Well into the nineteenth century, Sunday church services were held in the chambers of the Supreme Court and the House of Representatives. The Declaration of Independence appealed to "Nature's God," the "Creator," "the Supreme Judge of the World," and "divine Providence" for approval, legitimacy, and protection.

Rooted in Morality and Religion

The Constitution includes no such references. Yet its framers firmly believed that the republican government they were creating could only last if it was deeply rooted in morality and religion. "A Republic can only be supported by pure religion or austere morals," John Adams said. The Bible offers "the only system that ever did or ever will preserve a republic in the world." Washington agreed: "Reason and experience both forbid us to expect that national morality can prevail in exclusion of religious principles." The happiness of the people, good order, and civil government, declared the Massachusetts constitution of 1780, "essentially depend on piety, religion, and morality." Fifty years after the Constitution was adopted, [French historian Alexis de] Tocqueville reported that all Americans held religion "to be indispensable to the maintenance of republican institutions."

The words "separation of church and state" do not appear in the Constitution, and, as the historian Sidney Mead has pointed out, Madison spoke not of "church" and "state," European concepts with little relevance to America, but of "sects" and "Civil authority," and the "line" not the "wall" between them. Religion and society were coterminous.

Some people cite the absence of religious language in the Constitution and the provisions of the First Amendment as evidence that America is fundamentally a secular country. Nothing could be further from the truth. At the end of the eighteenth century, religious establishments existed throughout Europe and in several American states. Control of the church was a key element of state power, and the established church, in turn, provided legitimacy to the state. The framers of the American Constitution prohibited an established national church in order to limit the power of government and to protect and strengthen religion. The purpose of "separation of church and state," as William McLoughlin has said, was not to establish freedom from religion but to establish freedom for religion. It was spectacularly successful. In the absence of a state religion, Americans were not only free to believe as they wished but also free to create whatever religious communities and organizations they desired. As a result, Americans have been unique among peoples in the diversity of sects, denominations, and religious movements to which they have given birth, almost all embodying some form of Protestantism. When substantial numbers of Catholic immigrants arrived, it was eventually possible to accept Catholicism as one more denomination within the broad framework of Christianity. The proportion of the population who were "religious adherents," that is, church members, increased fairly steadily through most of American history. . . .

A Majority Affirms Belief in God

Today, overwhelming majorities of Americans affirm religious beliefs. When asked in 1999 whether they believed in God, or a universal spirit, or neither, 86 percent of those polled said they believed in God, 8 percent in a universal spirit, and 5 percent in neither. When asked in 2003 simply whether they believed in God or not, 92 percent said yes. In a series of 2002–03 polls, 57 to 65 percent of Americans said religion was very important in their lives, 23 to 27 percent said fairly important, and 12 to 18 percent said not very important. In 1996, 39 percent of Americans said they believed the Bible is the actual word of God and should be taken literally; 46 percent said they believed the Bible is the word of God but not everything in it should be taken literally word for word; 13 percent said it is not the word of God.

Large proportions of Americans also appear to be active in the practice of their religion. In 2002 and 2003, an average of 65 percent of Americans claimed membership in a church or synagogue. About 40 percent said they had attended church or synagogue in the last seven days. Roughly 33 percent said they went to church at least once a week, 10 percent almost every week, 15 percent about once a month, 27 percent seldom or a few times a year, and 15 percent never. In the same time period, about 60 percent of Americans said they prayed one or more times a day, more than 20 percent once or more a week, about 10 percent less than once a week, and 10 percent never. Given human nature, these claims of religious practice may be overstated, but even accounting for this factor, the level of religious activity was still high; and the extent to which Americans believe the right response is to affirm their religiosity is itself evidence for the centrality of religious norms in American society.

The Depth of American Religiosity

Reflecting on the depth of American religiosity, the Swedish theologian Krister Stendhal remarked, "Even the atheists in America speak in a religious key." Only about 10 percent of Americans, however, espouse atheism, and most Americans do not approve of it. A 1973 poll asked: "Should a socialist or an atheist be allowed to teach in a college or university?" The community leaders surveyed approved of both teaching. The American public as a whole agreed that socialists could teach (52 percent yes, 39 percent no), but decisively rejected the idea of atheists on college or university faculties (38 percent yes, 57 percent no). Since the 1930s, the willingness of Americans to vote for a Presidential candidate from a minority group has increased dramatically, with over 90 percent of those polled in 1999 saying they would vote for a black, Jewish, or female Presidential candidate, while 59 percent were willing to vote for a homosexual. Only 49 percent, however, were willing to vote for an atheist. Americans seem to agree with the Founding Fathers that their republican government requires a religious base, and hence they find it difficult to accept the explicit rejection of God and religion. . . .

Along with their general religiosity, the Christianity of Americans has also impressed foreign observers. There is no country in the world, Tocqueville said, where the Christian religion retains a greater influence over the souls of men than in America." Christianity, [English historian James] Bryce similarly observed, is "the national religion" of Americans. Americans have also affirmed their Christian identity. "We are a Christian people," the Supreme Court declared in 1811. The Senate Judiciary Committee echoed these words exactly in 1853, adding that "almost our entire population belong to or sympathize with some one of the Christian denominations." In the midst of the Civil War, Lincoln also described

Americans as "a Christian people." In 1892 the Supreme Court again declared, "This is a Christian nation." In 1908, a House of Representatives committee said that "the best and only reliance for the perpetuation of the republican institution is upon a Christian patriotism." In 1917 Congress passed legislation declaring a day of prayer in support of the war effort and invoking America's status as a Christian nation. In 1931 the Supreme Court reaffirmed its earlier view: "We are a Christian people, according to one another the equal right of religious freedom, and acknowledging with reverence the duty of obedience to the will of God."

Religiosity in the United States

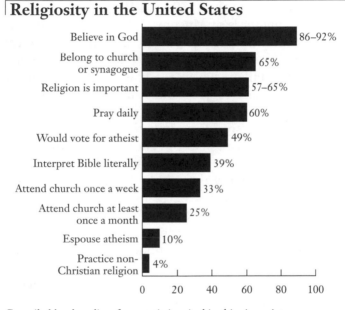

Compiled by the editor from statistics cited in this viewpoint.

While the balance between Protestants and Catholics shifted over the years, the proportion of Americans identifying themselves as Christian has remained relatively constant. In three surveys between 1989 and 1996, between 84 and 88 percent of Americans said they were Christians. The proportion of Christians in America rivals or exceeds the proportion of Jews in Israel, of Muslims in Egypt, of Hindus in India, and of Orthodox believers in Russia.

Debunking the Arguments

America's Christian identity has, nonetheless, been questioned on two grounds. First, it is argued that America is losing that identity because non-Christian religions are expanding in numbers, and Americans are thus becoming a multireligious and not simply a multidenominational people. Second, it is argued that Americans are losing their religious identity and are becoming secular, atheistic, materialistic, and indifferent to their religious heritage. Neither of these propositions comes close to the truth.

The argument that America is losing its Christian identity due to the spread of non-Christian religions was advanced by several scholars in the 1980s and 1990s. They pointed to the growing numbers of Muslims, Sikhs, Hindus, and Buddhists in American society. Hindus in America increased from 70,000 in 1977 to 800,000 in 1997. Muslims amounted to at least 3.5 million in 1997, while Buddhists numbered somewhere between 750,000 and 2 million. From these developments, the proponents of de-Christianization argue, in the words of Professor Diana Eck, that "religious diversity" has "shattered the paradigm of America" as an overwhelmingly Christian country with a small Jewish minority. Another scholar suggested that public holidays should be adjusted to accommodate this increasing religious diversity and that, for a start, it would be desirable to "have one Christian holiday (say, Christmas), but replace Easter and Thanksgiving with a Muslim and Jewish holiday." In some measure, however, the holiday trend was in the opposite direction. Hanukkah, "traditionally a minor Jewish holiday," has, according to Professor Jeff Spinner, been elevated into the "Jewish Christmas" and displaced Purim as a holiday, so as "to fit in better with the dominant culture."

The increases in the membership of some non-Christian religions have not, to put it mildly, had any significant effect on America's Christian identity. As a result of assimilation, low birth rates, and intermarriage, the proportion of Jews dropped from 4 percent in the 1920s to 3 percent in the 1950s to slightly over 2 percent in 1997. If the absolute numbers claimed by their spokesmen are correct, by 1997 about 1.5 percent of Americans were Muslim, while Hindus and Buddhists were each less than one percent. The numbers of non-Christian, non-Jewish believers undoubtedly will continue to grow, but for years to come they will remain extremely small. Some increases in the membership of non-Christian religions come from conversions, but the largest share is from immigration and high birth rates. The immigrants of these religions, however, are far outnumbered by the huge numbers of immigrants from Latin America and the Philippines, almost all of whom are Catholic and also have high birth rates. Latin American immigrants are also converting to evangelical Protestantism. In addition, Christians in Asia and the Middle East have been more likely than non-Christians to migrate to America. As of 1990, a majority of Asian Americans were Christian rather than Buddhist or Hindu. Among Korean Americans, Christians outnumber Buddhists by at least ten to one. Roughly one third of Vietnamese immigrants are Catholics. About two thirds of Arab Americans have been Christian rather than Muslim, although the number of Muslims was growing rapidly before September 11 [2001]. While a precise judgment is impossible, at the start of the twenty-first century the United States was probably becoming more rather than less Christian in its religious composition.

Tolerance for Religious Diversity

Americans tend to have a certain catholicity toward religion: All deserve respect. Given this general tolerance of religious diversity, non-Christian faiths have little alternative but to recognize and accept America as a Christian society. "Americans have always thought of themselves as a Christian nation" argues Jewish neoconservative Irving Kristol, "equally tolerant of all religions so long as they were congruent with traditional Judeo-Christian morality. But equal toleration . . . never meant perfect equality of status in fact." Christianity is not legally established, "but it is established informally, nevertheless." And, Kristol warns his fellow Jews, that is a fact they must accept.

But if increases in non-Christian membership haven't diluted Christianity in America, hasn't it been diluted, dissolved, and supplanted over time by a culture that is pervasively secular and irreligious, if not anti-religious? These terms describe segments of American intellectual, academic, and media elites, but not the bulk of the American people. American religiosity could still be high by absolute measures and high relative to that of comparable societies, yet the secularization thesis would still be valid if the commitment of Americans to religion declined over time. Little or no evidence exists of such a decline. The one significant shift that does appear to have occurred is a drop in the 1960s and 1970s in the religious commitment of Catholics. An overall fall off in church attendance in the 1960s was due to a decline in the proportion of Catholics attending mass every Sunday. In 1952, 83 percent of Catholics said that religion was very important in their lives; in 1987, 54 percent of Catholics said this. This shift brought Catholic attitudes on religion more into congruence with those of Protestants.

Over the course of American history, fluctuations did occur in levels of American religious commitment and religious involvement. There has not, however, been an overall downward trend in American religiosity. At the start of the twenty-first century, Americans are no less committed, and are quite possibly more committed, to their Christian identity than at any time in their history.

*"A large slice of the American public . . .
are living spiritual lives that are
customized [and] eclectic."*

Americans Are Adopting Nontraditional Approaches to Religion

Jesse Walker

A growing number of Americans are professing nontraditional religious beliefs, contends Jesse Walker in the following viewpoint. Some are members of mainstream religions who openly dispute the traditional doctrines of their faith; others adopt the practices of different faiths while remaining rooted in one tradition, Walker explains. Still others combine several religious traditions together or embrace new spiritual movements such as Wicca and neopaganism. The author concludes that members of mainstream religions are reshaping American society by challenging some of the traditions of their own belief systems. Walker is the associate editor of *Reason* magazine.

As you read, consider the following questions:

1. According to Walker, why does pro-choice activist Frances Kissling remain a Catholic even though she disagrees with the church's view on abortion?
2. How does Rabbi Schachter-Shalomi, quoted by the author, define "generic spirituality"?
3. How did neopaganism and Wicca develop, according to the author?

There is a group in the Dallas area called the Hot Tub Mystery Religion. Its adherents hold to no particular spiritual dogma, borrowing freely from such sources as Jewish mysticism, Roman paganism, Islamic heresy, and experimental art. One of its founders has compiled a recommended reading list for the faithful; it includes a collection of Tantric exercises, a text on Sufism, one of Philip K. Dick's Gnostic science fiction stories, and a novel by the Catholic apologist G.K. Chesterton. The group has been known to treat nitrous oxide as a sacrament and to throw Jacuzzi parties—hence the name.

In raw numbers, the Hottubbists constitute one of the smallest religions in the world: With well under 100 practitioners, it is dwarfed even by Rastafarianism and Scientology. The group is interesting for many reasons, but its social influence is not among them.

A Spiritual Cafeteria?

Though small and obscure, it is an example of a significant social trend: the blurring boundaries between art and faith. Atheists have long regarded religion as, at best, a collective work of art, but in the last century that view has grown popular with churchgoers as well. Many Christians and Jews today will declare that the Bible is a collection of myths and metaphors, not literal truths, and some will aver that there is more than one path to God. Neopagans and others take this nonliteral and eclectic approach and run with it, freely fusing classical mythologies, tribal spiritual practices, and even popular fiction, all of which would be mutually exclusive if they were regarded as, to borrow a phrase, the Gospel truth. At the far end of the spectrum are those who do not merely regard religion as a human creation but actively identify themselves as its creators. The Hot Tub group actually began as an art project, becoming a more spiritual endeavor only gradually. If it is unusual, it is only because it is so radical. Most people do not feel the need to be the authors of their own religions, though quite a few are happy to be the editors.

Whether this is bad or good depends on your attitude toward orthodoxy. Traditionalists often castigate what they call the spiritual cafeteria, in which ordinary worshippers pick and choose the beliefs and practices that appeal to them, customizing their faiths to fit their lifestyles instead of altering their lives to fit the dictates of their denominations. The cafeteria line includes every Catholic who casually dissents from the edicts of Rome, every otherwise observant Jew who eats food made in nonkosher kitchens, every Muslim who adjusts his prayer schedule to his workday rather than the other way around. Sometimes, these pickers and choosers even mix in their favorite features of other faiths.

Some think the most important religious trend today is a rise in fundamentalism; others, a rise in disbelief. But somewhere between those two phenomena, another interesting evolution is taking place. A large slice of the American public, many of them card-carrying members of mainline denominations, are living spiritual lives that are customized, eclectic, and otherwise comparable to those found in the Hot Tub church.

Customized Doctrine

Few issues seem more settled than the Vatican's position on abortion. The pope campaigns constantly against the practice, and the institution he heads has arguably done more for the fetal cause than any other group. The church's catechism—in its own words, "the essential and fundamental contents of Catholic doctrine"—declares, "Human life must be respected and protected absolutely from the moment of conception. From the first moment of his existence, a human being must be recognized as having the rights of a person—among which is the inviolable right of every innocent being to life."

So the first thing you might think, upon learning of a 30-year-old lobby called Catholics for a Free Choice (CFFC), is that its very premise is a paradox, comparable to Vegetarians for Veal or Maoists for the Preservation of Property Rights. Frances Kissling, the group's president since 1982, would disagree. "I have a good understanding of what I'm required to believe and accept as a Catholic," she says, "and I know that within the Catholic tradition, I have the right to dissent from even serious but non-infallible teachings. Abortion, women's ordination, family planning, married male priests, homosexuality: All these areas of controversy are open to disagreements." Pressed, she offers a detailed argument, part history and part theology, that the Catholic position on whether and when a fetus might be a person has varied considerably over the last two millennia.

I'm not competent to judge Kissling's theological position, and I'm not about to try. Her foes, however, have not been so wary. Magaly Llaguno, co-author of a tract titled *Catholics for a Free Choice Exposed*, has accused her of remaining in the church only "to sow discord and division." Speaking in Toronto in 1999, Llaguno said Kissling's group "is, in my opinion, usurping and misusing the term *Catholic*. Perhaps the Vatican and the bishops in each individual country in the world should copyright this term, so CFFC cannot continue to use it."

Private Belief Systems

Many Americans . . . are now cultivating highly personal forms of worship. What observers call "pastiche spirituality" or "religion à la carte" involves combining various beliefs and practices from different sources, or even being a member of two or more distinct religions at the same time. The possible variations are endless—and, as critics warn, so are the chances to lose one's way. Nevertheless, the land now abounds with these private belief systems, each tailored to fit the believer's individual needs.

Jeremiah Creedon, *Utne Reader*, July/August 1998.

Yet Kissling not only embraces the Catholic label but sees herself as part of a proud Roman tradition. She is a Catholic, not a Protestant, because something in Catholicism appeals to her. "There are parts of me that do say, 'Give it up, go someplace friendlier,'" she confesses. "But religious faith is not a matter of rationality. There's a part of my life, my spirit, that is irrational, and Catholicism appeals to that." She admires Catholicism's elaborate theology, its rich intellectual history, its support for humanitarian causes, even its music. ("I prefer Catholic Gregorian chants to Buddhist chants.") "It's partly cultural," she explains. "This is a religion I grew up with. I lived the first 20 years of my life in a largely Catholic community. Who I am—my values, how I see the world, my imagination—was formed by Catholicism. In the same way that I love myself, I love that which formed me."

Kissling adds that "even an excommunicated Catholic is a Catholic," which might strike even liberal clergy as going too far. Thus far she hasn't been expelled from the church, and she doesn't expect it to happen. But if that day ever comes, she plans to study the disputed doctrines one more time, to consult with her trusted colleagues, to pray, and then to "have the courage of what I think it means to be a Catholic—to say what I believe. And let the chips fall where they may."

The Many True Faiths

If that's a Catholic sentiment, it's one more at home in pluralist America than in, say, late-15th-century Spain. The rise of secular liberties has made it much easier to discard all or part of your faith without earthly repercussion, especially during the last century. At the same time, revolutions in communication and transportation have made it easier than ever to sample the planet's spiritual cuisines. A hundred and fifty years ago, an American could live his entire life without learning that Buddhism existed. Fifty years ago, in most of the country, he had to make a special effort to track down the details of Buddhist doctrine. Today, he can type a few words into a search engine and discover a host of Buddhisms, some more authentic than others.

If Kissling represents the first trend, then the second is embodied in Zalman Schachter-Shalomi, a Jew born in Austria and based today in Boulder, Colorado. The 78-year-old founder of the Alliance for Jewish Renewal is not merely a Hassidic rabbi but an initiated Sufi sheik; he has explored traditions ranging from Buddhism to voodoo, from Native American peyote rituals to the Baptist church. "In Judaism, we believe the messiah has not come yet," he says. "Which means we are not out of the woods yet, you know? We cannot claim that we have the totality of truth. Each of the religions has a fragment, and none of them has the whole thing."

A Common Truth

This universalist idea is hardly new. The Sufi philosopher Hazrat Inayat Khan, for one, argued a century ago that all the world's faiths shared a common truth. ("We need not give up our religion," he once wrote, "but we must embrace all religions in order to make the sacredness of religion perfect.") In 1923 Inayat initiated the Jewish-born Samuel Lewis, known to his followers as "Sufi Sam," who by that point was already well along a philosophical road whose stops ranged from Theosophy to Zen to General Semantics. It was Lewis, in turn, who initiated Schachter-Shalomi into Sufism. By that point, the rabbi had been venturing into other faiths for years.

Lewis' brand of Sufism does not claim to be Islamic. Schachter-Shalomi, by contrast, has never given up his Jewish roots. His explorations were meant not to replace the faith he was born into but to enrich and renew it. "Each time I would attend [another religion's services], I would learn something that would sharpen my own devotion," he says. "I would learn from the Quakers about sitting in silence, and I brought some of this to the synagogue. I would learn from the Baptists about praying outside of the prayer book, just from the heart. I would learn from the Christian Scientists to stand up and to give thanks for having been healed and helped." Echoing Inayat, Schachter-Shalomi argues that there is "an empirical reality that I call generic spirituality." Individual religions are merely fragments of that broader sense of the absolute, as refracted through "ethnic or historical components that gave it a particular flavor."

For all that, the rabbi doesn't entirely dismiss the traditionalist critique of the spiritual cafeteria. In the late '60s, when he sometimes taught in the San Francisco Bay area, he noticed that "people would say they were 'into' this now, and then they would get 'into' that, and each time they were looking for that honeymoon period with a new discipline." He corrects himself: "Not discipline—a new *tradition*. When it came to discipline, they'd opt out and then go to the next one. Because they wanted a *hit*."

The difference between them and him, he argues, is that "I didn't step out of Judaism to become a practicing something-else. But when I get in touch with another religion, and I attune to their dimension of the holy, I can bring that attunement back and enhance my connection to God."

If Kissling and Schachter-Shalomi seem avant-garde, it's only because they've thought through their positions with more rigor. If there aren't many Catholics with a detailed theological argument for abortion rights, there are plenty who break with their faith on that or some other important issue. And if Schachter-Shalomi's universalism is unusual, his willingness to explore rival confessions is not. Writing in *The Wall Street Journal* in 1999, Lisa Miller described not only the rabbi who became a Sufi sheik but a "Christian Buddhist, but sort of tongue-in-cheek," plus a Jewish/Buddhist cross-over that's "become so commonplace that marketers who sell spiritual books, videotapes and lecture series have a name for it: 'JewBu.'" Within the Unitarian Church, there are organizations of Unitarian Buddhists and even Unitarian Pagans.

Neopagans themselves mix all sorts of spiritual ingredients—and not always consciously. Many carry baggage from the churches they've supposedly rejected. "The former Catholics are the ones that are into the big ceremonial magic, because that's what they grew up with—the big Catholic ceremonies," argues Ceredwyn Alexander, a 33-year-old pagan (and former Catholic) who lives in Middlebury, Vermont. "And the Baptist pagans tend to be the rule-oriented pagans: 'You *must* be facing the east at this particular time of day, and anything other than that is evil and wrong!'"

Not every neopagan is as rigid as that. Indeed, neopaganism is almost unique among the world's faiths for its adherents' willingness not just to adopt radically new beliefs or practices but to jettison ideas that once stood at the center of the pagan worldview.

Wicca

Paganism in the broadest sense goes back to the Stone Age, but neopaganism is a product of the last 100 years, born when various mystics, most notably the English occultist Gerald Gardner, assembled new spiritual movements out of several preexisting social currents, from Freemasonry to woodcraft groups. Gardner claimed he had inherited his species of witchcraft, initially dubbed "Wica," from an unbroken chain of transmission that dated back to pre-Christian times, was kept alive in secret, and resurfaced publicly only after the U.K. repealed its anti-witchcraft statute in 1951. There are still some people who believe parts of that tale, but it is pretty well established by now that Wicca was Gardner's own invention.

This point is much less controversial in pagan circles than you might imagine. [In 2001], Charlotte Allen wrote an article for *The Atlantic* that was positively breathless in debunking Wicca's creation myths: that Gardner had revealed a long-established secret religion, that it could be traced back to a primeval goddess cult that once covered all of Europe, that the Christian witch hunts were launched to eradicate that ancient order, that this persecution was a holocaust that claimed 9 million women's lives. As Allen noted, the case for an overarching goddess-worshipping ur-faith has been severely weakened in recent years, while the rest of the story is in even worse shape: The figure of 9 million dead women is simply untrue, as is the notion of a witchy secret society that spent centuries underground.

How was Allen's article received? For the most part, to judge from the letters *The Atlantic* printed, with a been-there-done-that shrug. Toward the end of the piece, Allen herself eased up on the iconoclastic tone, allowing that many Wiccans "seem to be moving toward a position that accommodates, without exactly accepting," the new views.

That was an understatement. Pagan fundamentalists who insist their religion is centuries old certainly exist, but even in the 1970s mavericks such as Isaac Bonewitz, the Berkeley-based Druid, made a point of arguing that the Wiccan origin story was inaccurate. Margot Adler's *Drawing Down the Moon* (1979), one of the books that did the most to introduce Americans to neopaganism, frankly declared that until recently, most Wiccans "took almost all elements of the myth literally. Few do so today, which in itself is a lesson in the flexibility of the revival.". . .

The Evolution of a Religion

In *Triumph of the Moon* (1999), [British historian Ronald] Hutton argues that neopaganism is eclectic and protean. It is not just capable of adopting ideas—gods, rituals, creeds—from many different sources but is remarkably adaptable itself, allowing very different people to refashion it in their own images. This is true of all long-lived religions, of course, but in this case the evolution has occurred at a stunning pace.

Consider paganism's political dimensions. In *Modern Witchcraft* (1970), the journalist Frank Smyth observed that the British witches he interviewed tended to be politically conservative. So, Hutton notes, did the founders of the movement, and the figures who influenced them. But in the '60s and '70s—first in America, but soon in Britain as well—the religion was altered by feminist and environmentalist currents; in America especially, Wicca was often associated with the political left. The new collection *Modern Pagans* (2002), an anthology of interviews by V. Vale and John Sulak, reveals a subculture that would have been a bracing surprise to the neopagans of 50 years ago: goths, gay activists, anti-globalization protesters, a cyberspace-based "technopagan," even a Buddhist Beat poet.

It is the protean, adaptive quality Hutton identified that allowed these new variations to emerge. When feminists discovered paganism, they were attracted to the idea of goddess worship, and to the implications of a matriarchal past; the Wicca they then developed was very different from the one Gardner created. Green pagans, meanwhile, turned to "Earth-based spirituality"—and in the process, Hutton notes, they transformed fertility rites into nature worship. Libertarian pagans enjoyed the Millian overtones of Wicca's central ethical principle: "An it harm none, do as ye will.". . .

As one moves further from the Wiccan mainstream, neopaganism's eclectic quality—its status as a religion of appropriation—becomes yet more obvious. The Church of Aphrodite, founded on Long Island in 1938, was inspired by the myths of classical Greece as viewed through the lens of one Russian émigré's mind. Subsequent neopagans took their inspiration from the Druids, from ancient Egypt, from the Vikings, from Rome. Others looked to traditions that survived to the present day: to African animism, to Santeria and voodoo, to American Indian religions, even to Hinduism.

Inspiration does not mean perfect reconstruction. There is a sometimes dramatic difference between those in the original tradition and those appropriating it for their own purposes—between an ordinary Hindu, for example, and an American witch who has added the goddess Kali to her personal pantheon. One devotee of the Egyptian gods told Adler that he was a Jungian and that his deities "represent constructs—personifications." Some pagans would leave it at that; others, including Adler's interviewee, would insist that on the other side of those interpretive constructs are forces with an independent existence. Either way, it's a far cry from mainstream Hindu theology. . . .

Revised and Reinvented Faiths

In a way, none of this is unusual. There have always been people who discard the elements of their faith that they dislike, and there have always been syncretic religions that fuse one spiritual system with another. What is new is the ease of the former, the speed of the latter, and the extent to which the two have combined.

There is a wide gulf, of course, between someone who merely fine-tunes her Catholicism and someone who replaces the Virgin Mary with the goddess of chaos; between a Jew who mixes milk with meat and a Jew who practices witchcraft. If I am describing a trend, it is one that covers a wide spectrum of behavior, from the ordinary to the outré. As a journalist, I have naturally focused on the latter—but it's the former, obviously, that is reshaping society.

The question then becomes how adaptable these revised and reinvented faiths will be in the long haul. Rabbi Schachter-Shalomi notes that one function of religious ritual is to bind the generations, and that it's not clear how useful the new combinations are in that regard. "Most of the people who are inventing these things *de novo* will not have a second generation," he warns. "They wanted to get the highs out of the individual practice, but they don't do things in the household and families."

That doesn't mean that the spiritual cafeteria itself will inevitably collapse. More likely, the next generation will invent, reinvent, and rediscover its own religious practices, just as its parents are doing now.

"Religion, especially Christianity and to a lesser extent, Judaism, is increasingly subject to discrimination all over the United States."

Religious Believers Face Discrimination in America

Center on Religion and Society

In the viewpoint that follows, the Center on Religion and Society maintains that people of faith are facing escalating discrimination in the United States. Christians and Jews are increasingly denied the right to express their beliefs during religious holidays or to participate in public prayer. In addition, Christian commentators are strongly denounced in the mainstream media, the center reports. The author contends that if such discrimination continues, Christians are likely to abandon their efforts to improve society. The Center on Religion and Society is an organization that supports traditional Judeo-Christian values.

As you read, consider the following questions:

1. What does the author see as "fraudulent" about the way the First Amendment is interpreted today?
2. According to the author, why are the teachers in Libertyville, Illinois, forbidden to wear red and green pins during the Christmas season?
3. In what ways has antireligious discrimination favored Islam, in the author's view?

Center on Religion and Society, "Discrimination and Persecution," *Religion & Society Report*, vol. 20, May 2003, pp. 4–5. Copyright © 2003 by The Howard Center. Reproduced by permission.

It is becoming increasingly harder to close our eyes to the fact that religion, especially Christianity and to a lesser extent, Judaism, is increasingly subject to discrimination all over the United States and Western Europe. It has not yet reached the level of persecution, but it certainly is widespread and consistent. All of the symbols of Christianity are being forcibly removed from schools, public buildings, and government property. The interpretation of the First Amendment, called the separation of church and state, replaces the freedom of religion with freedom from and purging of religion. This fraudulent interpretation of the Amendment is now so familiar and well-established that it seems almost futile to criticize it, much less to attempt to change it.

The Silencing of Christians and Jews

When America accepts ever-growing numbers of immigrants from non-Christian cultures, does that automatically deprive the Christian majority of all rights of self-expression outside the private home? Does the fact that something that the majority cherishes may possibly offend a minority require that the majority relinquish all its symbolism? Should a tiny group of people claiming to be offended by stadium prayers in San Diego, Texas, prevent the vast majority of the audience from having a public prayer? Apparently so. A minority objects; the courts rule, and the Christians and, in some cases, the Jews are silenced.

In Deerfield, Illinois, the public library used to display a Christian creche and a menorah during the Christmas season (forgive us, the holiday season). The raising of an objection by a contentious atheist from nearby Buffalo Grove resulted in the library director ordering the removal of everything reminiscent of the season, which is now just the "winter holiday." In Libertyville, Illinois, the school board has forbidden the teachers to wear red and green pins and other decorations that might cause children to ask, "Why are you wearing that?" Sometimes a kind of political correctness prevails, creating a reversal of anti-religious discrimination in favor of Islam; [in the fall of 2002], the University of North Carolina at Chapel Hill required incoming freshmen to read a book with a very positive treatment of Islam, while in California, an elementary school required students to pretend that they were Muslims, dressing accordingly and reciting Muslim prayers.

Anti-Christian Scorn

I am well-acquainted with the Christian Right both from travel and from my own associations as a Christian. But I've also taught at the University of Texas at Austin since 1983, so I have a sense of the intellectual leanings of my liberal-to-radical faculty colleagues and distinctly progressive hometown. These parties typically define Christianity in terms of the sins committed in its name, which is like defining science in terms of those who have rigged experiments or used discoveries to create weapons of mass destruction.

This faulty view of Christianity is far from benign. In fact, it has sparked a new wave of religious bigotry in this country. . . . Many leading American thinkers . . . speak of Bible-believing Christians the way earlier establishments spoke about Jews. They vent their scorn in Georgetown salons and at Manhattan dinner parties, and their attitudes are evident in media treatment of religion and America's people of faith.

Marvin Olasky, *American Outlook*, Summer 2000.

At the University of North Carolina in Charlotte, commencement ceremonies go by without any invocation, prayers, or thanksgiving to God, although thanks are expressed to the teachers, the school, the state, and almost anything else except Mickey Mouse. This is in a state with a strongly Christian population and huge Christian churches, both liberal and conservative, and as little as a few years ago such a ceremony without prayers of thanksgiving to God would have been unthinkable.

Criticism of Christian Thinkers

Serious Christian writers such as Pat Robertson, Jerry Falwell, and Franklin Graham, the son of evangelist Billy Graham, are regularly denounced in the supposedly objective media, even on the news pages, with an intensity seldom used even on the most vigorous of the political conservatives, Pat Buchanan. The scandal involving pedophile priests that broke [in 2002] and that ultimately resulted in the defrocking of Boston archbishop Bernard Cardinal Law, may have received less attention than otherwise might have been heaped upon it, because it soon came out that most of the offenses were homosexual in nature rather than heterosexual.

None of this constitutes actual persecution, but it is discouraging to and wearing upon Christians who constantly have to put up with being reduced to the status of less than second-class citizens, as well as rather public nuisances. If there is to be a national revival, it will surely have to have a religious component, and most of that component will be Christian. Unfortunately, the discriminatory policies of government and the media may gradually dispel the desire of Christians to do anything positive in society.

| *"Nonbelievers are the most unjustly despised minority in the United States today."*

Nonbelievers Face Discrimination in America

Edward Tabash

Edward Tabash is a constitutional lawyer working in Beverly Hills, California; he is also a member of the board of directors of the Council for Secular Humanism. In the year 2000 Tabash was the only known secular humanist to have been a candidate for a state legislature. In the following viewpoint Tabash argues that nonbelievers face significant discrimination in the United States. This bias is evident in polls revealing that a large percentage of Americans would vote against a candidate just for being an atheist and in the negative public response to atheists' efforts to ensure equal treatment for all people regardless of belief. Tabash contends that attempts by atheists and humanists to achieve equal status constitute a genuine civil rights movement.

As you read, consider the following questions:

1. What percentage of Americans would vote against an atheist on the grounds of atheism alone, according to a poll cited by Tabash?
2. According to the author, what percentage of Americans favor restoring government-sponsored prayer in public schools?
3. What does Tabash propose that nonbelievers do to forward the interests of their community?

Edward Tabash, "Atheism Is Indeed a Civil Rights Issue," *Free Inquiry*, vol. 24, June/July 2004, pp. 44–45. Copyright © 2004 by Council for Democratic and Secular Humanism, Inc. Reproduced by permission.

O ne test of whether a minority group's struggle for equality is a civil rights issue is whether majority attitudes toward that minority reflect unreasonable prejudice or a desire to deny full legal rights to its members. By this standard, atheists' efforts to achieve legal and social equality indeed constitute a civil rights movement. Consider that, in 1958, a Gallup poll revealed that 53 percent of American citizens would vote against a Black candidate for president on grounds of race alone. In a 1999 Gallup poll, that figure had declined to 4 percent. That same 1999 Gallup poll revealed that a larger percentage of American citizens, 49 percent, would vote against an atheist *on grounds of atheism alone* than would vote against someone for any other reason. Even though this is the lowest comparative percentage of people who said they would vote against someone just for being a nonbeliever, in absolute numbers, it is still a higher percentage than is applicable to any other historically disfavored group.

Opposition to Nonbelievers

Given current attitudes, new laws that overtly discriminate against atheists would pass easily, and any such existing laws would eagerly be enforced—save only for the United States Supreme Court, which has held consistently since 1947 that no branch of government can favor believers over nonbelievers. Enlightened as this position may be, it has *never* enjoyed majority support. Quite to the contrary, each time the Supreme Court, indeed any court, has struck down government preference for religion over nonbelief, an overwhelming majority of the public has opposed the decision in question.

Ever since the famous Supreme Court rulings of 1962 and 1963 that ended teacher-led prayer and Bible readings in public schools, in poll after poll Americans have favored returning government sponsored prayer to public schools by a *minimum* margin of 69 percent to 27 percent. In many surveys, the percentage favoring restoration of school prayer exceeds 75 percent.

In other words, an overwhelming majority of Americans *rejects* the offer of fairness that atheists and secular humanists have always proposed. We don't want government to favor us over others; we just want government to be neutral, so that both believers and nonbelievers will be equal before the law. We want government to stay out of the God controversy, so that the official structure of society equally embraces both believers and nonbelievers. We want government to be silent on the question of God's existence and on matters of worship. Even a moderate conservative like U.S. Supreme Court Justice Sandra Day O'Connor has endorsed this position, asserting that the First Amendment prohibits all branches of government from treating people differently based upon "the God or gods they worship or don't worship."

In contrast, most Americans yearn for government to take sides in the dispute over whether God exists. And so, we atheists and humanists find ourselves dependent on a constitutional mandate of equality before the law, the immediate survival of which depends upon a dangerously narrow margin of *just two votes* on the Supreme Court. A shift of these two votes would establish a five-vote majority on the Court sufficient to abolish the present requirement of government neutrality between religion and nonbelief. So far, President [George W.] Bush has succeeded in appointing judges to the lower federal courts who openly favor a Christian theological basis for our legal system. These judges, unfortunately reflecting attitudes held by most Americans, maintain that the Supreme Court has been wrong in its unbroken line of decisions that require government to treat belief and nonbelief equally.

An Unjustly Despised Minority

Since the majority in our nation regards nonbelievers with disdain and craves an end to government neutrality between religion and nonbelief, the struggle of atheists in the United States is indeed a civil rights issue. But that's not the worst of it.

Mainstream Americans don't simply reject atheism. Far too many of them also revile atheists, secular humanists, and other unbelievers *as persons*. In reflecting upon my own narrow loss in my 2000 bid for a seat in the California legislature, I have written that nonbelievers are the most unjustly despised minority in the United States today.

History and current events confirm how sharply nonbelievers are loathed. Consider the torrent of hatred today directed toward Michael Newdow, the courageous plaintiff in the effort to remove "under God" from the Pledge of Allegiance that public school children are expected to recite. Far from being unusual, the negative public response toward Newdow *typifies* the rage with which most Americans respond when anyone from our community demands that official government pronouncements be as equally inclusive of us as they are of everyone else.

Wasserman. © 2000 by *Boston Globe*. Reproduced by permission.

Or consider a historical example. In February 1964, when the landmark Civil Rights Act was being debated in Congress, the House of Representatives passed a measure by a vote of 137 to 98 that *explicitly excluded atheists* from protection under the new law that would otherwise abolish employment discrimination. Fortunately, the measure failed in the Senate. Still, just forty years ago, the same House of Representatives that declared it illegal to engage in employment discrimination against African Americans was willing to give employers free rein to go on discriminating against people who didn't believe in God.

A Civil Rights Struggle

I submit that bigotry against a person just because that individual rejects unproven supernatural claims is every bit as destructive of the quest for a just and enlightened society as is bigotry against someone on grounds of race or ethnicity.

To the extent that a clear majority of Americans, let alone an overwhelming majority, *wants* government at all levels to officially favor religion over nonbelief—to the extent that more Americans still view atheism as a disqualifying characteristic in a political candidate than they do any other factor—I submit that we nonbelievers are in just as much danger of suffering open discrimination as is the gay community. Even though there have not yet been any notable physical attacks on atheists—just for being atheists—discrimination does not have to be accompanied by overt violence in order to pose a grave threat to a minority group's struggle for full equality. Further, if President Bush succeeds in restructuring the Supreme Court so as to create a majority willing to nullify church/state separation, open discrimination against atheists and secular humanists may become the active and enforceable law of the land.

Accordingly, the efforts of atheists, secular humanists, and other nonbelievers to secure and preserve their equality before the law is every bit as much a civil rights struggle as is that of the gay rights movement.

Should Atheists Elect Their Own?

One of the most important advances members of any unjustly despised minority can make is to begin electing members of their own community to political office. Consider how pathetically contemporary politicians pander to religion—for example, when *every* United States senator gathered on the Capitol steps to support "under God" in the Pledge of Allegiance after the initial Ninth Circuit finding favorable to Newdow was announced. Clearly our best protection against legislation hostile to nonbelievers would be to get some atheists elected to Congress and state legislatures.

[Some critics] reproach what they portray as my stance that atheists should vote for an atheist candidate solely because of his or her atheism. My actual position is that, given the dearth of nonbelievers currently holding significant political office in the United States, when one of our colleagues in freethought makes a bid for office and has a significant chance of winning, we should try to give that candidate our support even if we do not agree with him or her on every issue. We nonbelievers can be a contentious lot, often withholding our backing from anyone with whom we disagree on even just one issue. As a practical matter, we will never find a candidate with whom we agree on everything. My suggestion, then, is for atheists and secular humanists to try to give a viable candidate from our own community greater leeway on topics not directly germane to the equal rights of nonbelievers and church-state separation. Each of us should try to support that candidate, unless he or she holds a position on some issue that violates one of our core individual beliefs.

The gay community, women, African Americans, and other minority groups have learned the importance of civil rights activism, and of electing their own to political office. Since the mood of the country is so antagonistic toward atheists, our own quest to secure and preserve equality before the law is clearly a civil rights issue. As such, just like any other unjustly despised minority, we must learn how to elect a number of our own to the halls of power.

Periodical Bibliography

The following articles have been selected to supplement the diverse views presented in this chapter.

Clark D. Adams	"My Cup Is Half Full: Why I Am Optimistic About the Rights of Nonbelievers," *Freethought Today*, October 2002.
Forrest Church	"The American Creed," *Nation*, September 16, 2002.
Stephen Cox	"The Romance of the New Religions," *Liberty*, February 2003.
Julia Duin	"Americans Keep Faith, Lose Religion," *Insight on the News*, May 27, 2002.
Samuel P. Huntington	"American Creed: How Our Spiritual Heritage Shaped Our National Identity," *American Conservative*, April 12, 2004.
Joe Lieberman	"Vision for America: A Place for Faith," *Responsive Community*, Winter 2000–2001.
Michael Novak	"A Nation That Believes: America Without Religion Is Not America," *National Review*, December 31, 2001.
Jonathan Rauch	"Let It Be: The Greatest Development in Modern Religion Is Not Religion at All—It's an Attitude Best Described as 'Apatheism,'" *Atlantic Monthly*, May 2003.
Roy Speckhardt	"'Nonreligious' People Figure Strongly in the United States," *Humanist*, January/February 2002.
John G. Stackhouse Jr.	"Where Religion Matters," *American Outlook*, Fall 2002.
Cal Thomas	"Are Christians Persecuted or Just Too Tightly Wound?" *Los Angeles Times*, November 21, 1999.
Jay Tolson	"The Faith of Our Fathers," *U.S. News & World Report*, June 28, 2004.
Alan Wolfe and Michael Cromartie	"'Salvation Inflation?' A Conversation with Alan Wolfe," *Books & Culture*, March/April 2004.
Cathy Young	"Beyond Belief: When Will Secularism Be Allowed in the Public Square?" *Reason*, October 2004.

What Effect Does Religion Have on American Society?

Chapter Preface

In 1996 a group formed to organize citizens in the greater Boston area across racial, ethnic, class, and neighborhood lines. Its goal was to initiate actions that would help solve local community and economic problems. Over the course of several years, the group's participants made great strides: They secured 23 million dollars in new funding for affordable housing from the city of Boston, they won a 2-million-dollar increase in funding for textbooks and instructional supplies for local schools, and they coorganized a campaign to win significant pay and benefit increases for the area's poorly paid janitors. The organization is not a political advocacy group, a union, or a legal foundation. It is the Greater Boston Interfaith Organization (GBIO), a coalition of clergy, diverse religious congregations, community leaders, and other civic organizations.

Many policy makers point to groups like the GBIO as examples of religion's beneficial effects on American society. As Joe Loconte, a research fellow for the Heritage Foundation, contends, religious groups are making significant progress in many communities in alleviating or preventing social problems such as crime, substance abuse, illiteracy, and poverty. Loconte believes that the religious motivations of faith-based organizations are integral to their success. "The best social-science research confirms what common sense suggests," he explains. "Active religious congregations are a critical factor in reducing violence and stabilizing inner-city neighborhoods." The influence of religion is often indirect, observers point out. As Loconte maintains, a study conducted by the National Bureau of Economic Research "found that urban youth whose neighbors attend church are more likely to have a job and less likely to use drugs or commit crime."

Other analysts, however, are more cautious about lauding the benefits of religion and the successes of faith-based organizations. Jacob S. Hacker, a researcher for the New America Foundation, wonders whether religious organizations can be as effective as government or professional secular organizations in providing for the social welfare of people in need. "To ascribe to faith-based organizations a magical power to

heal all social ills is to forget how limited their resources are
. . . and how extensively their success depends on a steady
supply of public funds and interactions with government
agencies. It is also to forget that the strength of many of these
institutions rests precisely on their voluntary character—and
on their ability to advance beliefs that are sectarian, exclusionary, and even offensive to some." Lawyer and critic
Wendy Kaminer agrees and questions the notion that organized religion has positive social benefits or moralizing effects: "Considering the persistence of religious bigotry, not
to mention the history of religious warfare, it is a bit perverse
to promote religion as an antidote for social disorder."

In December 2002 President George W. Bush issued an
executive order that granted religious social service providers
greater access to federal funding. In the years to come, the
question of whether religion and faith-motivated groups help
to ease social problems will remain a subject of debate as researchers gather data pertaining to this issue. The authors in
the following chapter offer additional perspectives on the effect of religion on American society and discuss the often
volatile relationship between religion and politics.

"Christians are living holy lives that are having an enormous impact within our society."

Religion Benefits America

Leith Anderson

Religion, particularly Christianity, has positively affected American society, argues Leith Anderson in the following viewpoint. It was the influence of Christianity that led to the abolition of slavery, the author points out. Over the course of the nation's history, furthermore, Christianity helped to bring about a general reduction in drug abuse, political corruption, and immorality, states Anderson. Although America still faces difficulties, Christians who remain rooted in their faith offer stability and guidance, Anderson concludes. Anderson is the pastor of Wooddale Church in Eden Prairie, Minnesota, and author of *Leadership That Works: Hope and Direction for Church and Parachurch Leaders in Today's Complex World.*

As you read, consider the following questions:

1. According to Anderson, which national leaders have publicly stated that they are born-again Christians?
2. What percentage of Americans describe themselves as Christians, according to the author?
3. What message does the parable of the wheat and the weeds have for Christians today, in Anderson's opinion?

Leith Anderson, "The Christian Future of America: Two Views: Has the Nation Finally Abandoned Its Judeo-Christian Heritage, or Is There Still Hope?" *Christianity Today*, vol. 48, August 2004, pp. 38–42. Copyright © 2004 by Leith Anderson. Reproduced by permission.

I spoke at a convention in Philadelphia where, after one of my sessions, a woman raised her hand and asked, "If the gospel and the church are supposed to be so effective, why is everything in America so bad?"

What she was saying, basically, is that the gospel of Jesus Christ doesn't work. And perhaps the reason she assumes that failure is because she has heard that message so often from our pulpits, our broadcasts, and our publications. The gospel might have worked somewhere else. It might have worked at another time. But we are repeatedly told that the gospel doesn't work anymore; we have had ample opportunity in America for the gospel to have significant impact, but what we often hear is that things are getting far worse.

So how bad are things in the United States? Indeed, we live in difficult times. Not one of us needs to look very far to see the effects of sin. We have corporate corruption, pornography, abortions, divorces, anemic churches, 5 million couples living together who are not married, clergy immorality, drug abuse, and more.

But that really isn't anything new, is it? In the history of America, the roots of deism and secularism go back a long way. Books like *Undaunted Courage*, about the Lewis and Clark expedition, and *Theodore Rex*, the biography of Theodore Roosevelt, remind us of the appalling immorality, drug abuse, and business and political corruption that permeated generations 100 and 200 years ago.

So things have been bad, and continue to be bad, in lots of ways. But what kind of influence are Christians having on our country today?

The Difference Christians Make

One hundred and fifty years ago, slavery became illegal in America when abolitionist Christians put their lives on the line for human freedom. One hundred years ago in America, opium, laudanum (an opium-based painkiller), and morphine use was so pervasive that it produced an unprecedented number of addicts. One hundred years ago, the Sears and Roebuck catalog sold heroine and syringes through the mail. Fifty years ago theological liberalism dominated the religious landscape of America, and born-again Christians were clearly on the margins of society.

Today, those who publicly state that they are born-again Christians include the President of the United States, the attorney general, the national security adviser, governors of many states, members of Congress, senators, CEOs of our largest corporations, university professors, best-selling authors like John Grisham, country music stars like Randy Travis—on and on the list goes.

New York City had a reputation a generation ago for being one of the dirtiest and most unsafe cities in the world. Today it has one of the lowest crime rates, per capita, in the country. More than three-quarters of Americans describe themselves as Christians. Churches where the Bible is taught and holiness is lived are multiplying and flourishing. The largest and most effective churches in America, almost without exception, have a serious commitment to the truth of the Bible and the authority of Jesus Christ.

There are fewer R-rated films produced now than there were 10 years ago. And one of the most successful R-rated films is *The Passion of the Christ*. The best-selling books in America, and around the world, in recent years have included *The Prayer of Jabez, Left Behind*, and *The Purpose-Driven Life*.

I remember well when pornography magazines were sold in 7-Eleven and other convenience stores. I don't recommend that you go and look for them, but you would have difficulty finding those publications readily available in those stores today.

The *New York Times* editorialized recently that evangelical Christians in America are shaping U.S. foreign policy toward righteousness.

And on it goes. Christians are living holy lives that are having an enormous impact within our society.

A Deep Faith

Some Christian leaders say that Christianity in America is, in fact, 3,000 miles wide and one inch deep. As someone who travels a great deal in this country and interacts across the nation on a weekly basis with Christians, I simply say, that's not my experience.

One way to test that theory is to take out the sharp knife of tragedy and cut deep to see what's under an inch of American Christianity. I remember the day of tragedy at Columbine High School.[1] My wife, Charleen, and I walked the perimeter of the fence and saw the thousands upon thousands of notes and little shrines that were established. We spent hours reading them, and almost all of them acknowledged a loyalty to God and a love for Jesus Christ.

I was commuting to a job in Washington, D.C., when the sniper tragedies were taking lives at random around the metropolitan area.[2] And I watched carefully on television when people who were absolutely shaken by the tragic deaths of family members stated that their only hope and confidence was in Jesus Christ and that Jesus Christ had given them strength, stability, and peace in the midst of their difficulties.

Varvel. © by Gary Varvel. Reproduced by permission.

[The terrorist attacks of] September 11, 2001, produced more testimonies to Jesus Christ than anything that I can remember in recent times.

1. On April 20, 1999, two students shot and killed twelve schoolmates and a teacher at this Colorado high school before killing themselves.   2. In October 2002, ten people were killed and three wounded in a series of sniper attacks in the Washington, D.C., area.

On September 29 [2003], there was a shooting in a Hennepin County Courthouse in the Twin Cities in Minnesota. A severely wounded attorney lay bleeding on the floor of the courthouse hallway. The *Minneapolis Star Tribune* in a front-page story told about the woman who knelt down in front of this man. She pressed her navy blue suit jacket so hard against the wound on his neck that her arm shook. "Jesus, please save this man," she prayed over and over. "Jesus, don't let this man die."

Listen to a Real Cynic

We often hear cynical Christians condemn the impotence of American Christianity, but listen to a real cynic: Justin Webb, the BBC correspondent in Washington, D.C. He spoke about his postings in Belgium, London, and then the United States.

> My wife and I do not believe in God. In our first posting in Brussels among the nominally Catholic Belgians, unbelief was not a problem. Our house in London was right next to a church. We talked to the tiny congregation about the weather, about the need to prune the rosebushes and mend the fence, but we never talked about God. How different it is here on this side of the Atlantic.
>
> I'm not talking about the Bible Belt—or about the loopy folk who live in log cabins in Idaho and Oregon and worry that the government is poisoning their water. I'm talking about Mr. and Mrs. Average in Normal Town, U.S.A. Mr. and Mrs. Average share an uncomplicated faith with its roots in the Puritanism of [their] forebears. According to that faith there is such a thing as heaven—86 percent of Americans, we are told by the pollsters, believe in heaven.
>
> But much more striking for me and much more pertinent to current world events is that 76 percent, or three out of four people you meet on any American street, believe in hell and the existence of Satan. They believe the devil is out to get you, that evil is a force in the world—a force to be engaged in battle. Much of the battle takes place in the form of prayer. Americans will talk of praying as if it were the most normal, rational thing to do. The jolly plump woman who delivers our mail in the Washington suburbs has a son who is ill—the doctors are doing their best, she says, but she's praying hard and that's what will do the trick.

And so I'll tell you, I'm awed. I'm impressed and awed by

Christians in America who in facing unexpected tragedies turn to God.

Growing Wheat

Jesus' parable of the wheat and the weeds in Matthew 13 is fitting for us who live in the best of times and the worst of times. Servants asked the master whether they should tear out the weeds that had unexpectedly grown up alongside the wheat. The master replied no: "Because while you are pulling the weeds you may root up the wheat with them. Let both grow together until the harvest. At that time I will tell the harvesters, first collect the weeds and tie them into bundles to be burned and then gather the wheat and bring it into my barn."

Let there be no doubt, wheat and weeds are growing side by side in America. But Jesus tells his followers not to worry about pulling up the weeds—he will take care of that later. Instead he tells his followers to grow the wheat.

"It is the ignorance fostered by religion that now threatens our very species with extinction."

Religion Harms America

Frank R. Zindler

Religion is a serious threat to America's national institutions and to the human species, contends Frank R. Zindler in the following viewpoint. The dangers of religion can be seen in the decisions made by President George W. Bush, an evangelical Christian who is woefully ignorant of science, Zindler argues. Bush has, for example, made choices that are intensifying the problems of pollution, population growth, and environmental destruction. Because religious belief is at the root of scientific ignorance, religion must be extracted from U.S. governmental institutions and replaced with reason and sanity, the author concludes. Zindler is the editor of *American Atheist*, a quarterly journal. This viewpoint was delivered as a speech before the Godless Americans March on Washington in 2002.

As you read, consider the following questions:
1. What was the Enlightenment, according to Zindler?
2. According to the author, how has President George W. Bush impaired population control efforts in the third world?
3. What is the "job of religion," in Zindler's opinion?

Frank R. Zindler, "A Government in Thrall to Religion," *American Atheist*, vol. 41, Winter 2002–2003, pp. 14–15. Copyright © 2003 by *American Atheist*. Reproduced by permission.

The government of the United States of America kneels in thrall to religion. Priests and preachers have triumphed over the Constitution of our country.

The wall of separation between state and church has not only been mined, sapped, and breached by the forces of superstition, the parts of it that remain appear to be about to be incorporated into the walls of a church—a state church.

With the victory of faith-based forces, science and learning—the age-old victims of religion—now face a danger such as they have not seen since the time of the Holy Roman Inquisition.

The Threat to Science

The threat to science posed by religion is a peril to us all, for it is science that has been our great benefactor, liberator, and secular savior. It is science that has buoyed us up over the dark and swelling tide of superstition, faith, and ignorance, and has carried us to within sight of a world more beautiful by far than any paradise conjured in the ancient dreams of primitive priests.

It is not only our liberty for which we must fear if religion consummates its conquest of the Capitol, the White House, and the Supreme Court. Our very lives and those of our descendants are in jeopardy.

Given the grave environmental dangers confronting a species that has soiled its nest—a species that has multiplied beyond the carrying capacity of the spaceship it calls Earth—facts, facts, and more facts relating to the problem must be discovered, evaluated, and used to find solutions that will allow the survival of *Homo sapiens*.

The fantasies and prayers of religion simply will not do. Nothing fails like prayer.

If a government relies upon a god, who can rely upon that government to find solutions to the world's problems? If elected officials believe in an undetectable world beyond the reach of science, who can trust their judgment in the real world?

Since science is the only antidote to the lethally wishful thinking of religion, it is worrisome to the edge of terrifying to discover that the chief executive of this great nation is woefully ignorant of science. Although these United States of America are the fruit of the period known as the Enlightenment—a period when religion was subjected to scientific study and many had cast off its shackles—they are now governed by an Evangelist-in-Chief rather than by a scientist and discoverer of truth such as Thomas Jefferson.

The man who has his finger on the button that could launch a nuclear Armageddon cannot even pronounce the word 'nuclear.' Worse yet, his mispronunciation of the word *nuclear* would seem to signal the total depth of his understanding of physics.

Humanity in Peril

The threat to us all from this embarrassing situation would not be so grave if the president had realized the danger in his disability and had surrounded himself with competent scientific advisers. But alas, his very ignorance of science has prevented him from realizing the urgency of seeking good scientific advice. Formerly, the national science adviser, as head of the White House Office of Science and Technology Policy, held a near-cabinet-level position with the title "Assistant to the President." Dr. John H. Marburger, the president's adviser, does not have such a title nor does he have much clout with his chief. An executive order simply refers to him as a "Federal Government official."

At first, when George W. Bush came to power, it seemed there might not be a science adviser at all, and it was not until October 23, 2001—nine months later—that Dr. Marburger was confirmed. This initial disdain of science has translated into a number of actions which have put us and the whole human race in peril.

The Web-site of Health and Human Services [HHS] and the NIH [National Institutes of Health] have yielded to radical religious pressure and have removed important information relating to reproductive health.

David Hager, author of *Stress and a Woman's Body*, a book that promotes "the restorative power of Jesus Christ in one's life," has been appointed chairman of the Health Drugs Advisory Committee of the Food and Drug Administration.

The Bush administration has stacked an advisory panel on

childhood lead poisoning with lead industry allies. Apparently thinking scientific truth can be voted on, Claude Allen, deputy secretary of HHS explains this shocking situation by noting, "in getting broad views . . . we think industry has a voice and should have a voice."

Why *shouldn't* we set foxes to guard our hen houses?

The president has deprived the U.N. Population Fund of $34 million dollars. This will gravely impair population control efforts in the Third World, where 80 million pregnancies per year are unwanted.

A Distrust of Science

The need for a strong secularist defense of science is especially urgent, because many of the religious right's policy goals are intimately linked to a profound distrust of science and scientists. There is a strong connection between the revival of antievolutionism since 1980 and the attack on separation of church and state, because the Christianization of secular public education has long been a goal of the forces of conservative religions.

There is also a link between the antievolution campaign and the general decline of American scientific literacy. During the past two decades, study after study has documented the declining knowledge of basic scientific facts among American public school students and their teachers. This ignorance is generally attributed to lax American education standards, and there is of course a great deal of truth in the charge. But fundamentalist, antimodernist religion has also been a significant player in the dumbing down of the elementary and secondary school science curriculum.

Susan Jacoby, *Nation*, April 19, 2004.

The Bush administration has sided with polluters. It has given the green light to arsenic pollution, air pollution, and water pollution.

Again and again, advisors who should be selected for their scientific expertise are being chosen for their ideology and ties to Bush-friendly industries.

Mr. Bush pulled out of the Kyoto Accord (an international treaty on global warming), since he doesn't believe global warming is a reality.

Perhaps the greatest scientific discovery of our president

is his finding that the best way to prevent forest fires is to cut down the trees.

The EPA [Environmental Protection Agency] is now allowing mining companies to dump waste into America's rivers and streams.

Mr. Bush has announced a rollback of power plant pollution rules that will allow more mercury, sulfur, and nitrogen oxide emissions.

In his original budget, the president cut funding for research and development of renewable energy sources by approximately half.

Bush's blueprint for NASA [National Aeronautics and Space Administration] involves discontinuation of priority remote sensing and environmental application projects.

He cut the budget of the US Geological Survey by 22%.

On August 9, 2001, President Bush placed crippling restrictions on research done with embryonic human stem cells.

The president also wants to outlaw human cloning of any kind—both reproductive and therapeutic.

Therapeutic cloning potentially is the greatest breakthrough in the history of medical science. It offers a prospect of practical immortality. President Bush, like the angel who chased Adam and Eve from the Garden of Eden, does not want us to have a chance to eat the fruit of the tree of life.

The Dangers of Ignorance

Certainly, Mr. Bush's most generous campaign supporters will benefit from his antienvironmental decisions, and the priests and preachers who supplied him with votes will benefit by the harm he has done to health and reproductive programs and research.

But can all the president's actions be explained as simply the product of greed and self-interest? I don't think he is really *that* evil. Rather, I think his ignorance of science allows him—with a clean conscience—to harm the environment and block our prospects for life-saving medical breakthroughs.

He knoweth not what he doeth. If he had a firm grasp of the science of ecology, he would realize that his children and later descendants are imperiled by planet-wide pollution, by destruction of forests, by runaway population growth, and by greenhouse warming of the earth.

He can collude with greedy and conscienceless corporations because he does not understand the reality of climate change and the dire ecological consequences of Earth's warming.

He doesn't understand that ecologists are scientists. He thinks they are just wacko tree-hugging bird-watching eccentrics who don't understand economics. He is unaware that economics is simply a subdiscipline of ecology.

If the president could understand how overpopulation is a major contributor to the strife and violence so rampant in the world today, he could not have caved in to the pope and withheld funding for the UN population fund.

If the president realized that acorns are not oak trees, he would not be trying to suppress abortion rights.

If he understood that embryos are not persons, he would not oppose therapeutic cloning, a technique that potentially could allow us indefinitely to replace worn-out body parts and give us a shot at practical immortality.

Alas, our president is so uninformed on this subject, he thinks mad cloners would be producing identical twins of people who would probably be kept in some laboratory limbo and mined for body parts.

The Job of Religion

Scientific ignorance is the root of most of the problems facing us at the beginning of this new millennium, and we must not forget that it is the job of religion to keep America ignorant. Priests and preachers are secure in power only if their minions are ignorant of everything except the self-serving propaganda fed them by their brain-washers.

It is the ignorance fostered by religion that now threatens our very species with extinction. It is this ignorance that has gained control of our federal government. This ignorance must be dispelled.

This ignorance must be expelled from the governmental side of the wall that once separated the state from the church in this dear land. Only by expelling religion from the government of this nation can we repair the damage done by the failure of reality testing that it has fostered.

What Godless Americans Must Do

A burden has fallen upon us—the godless Americans. . . .

It is we who must restore America to the status of being "one nation under the Constitution" instead of "one nation under God."

It is we who must bring the enlightenment of science into governments—governments all the way from school boards to the White House. . . .

In the long line of generations stretching into the unmeasured prehistoric past, no generation has been saddled with so heavy a responsibility as that which we must now assume.

Never before have the stakes been so high. Never before has the penalty for inaction been so horrific. We might not have a second chance.

Religion has slipped a Trojan Horse into the public barn, so that priests secreted inside can feed at monetary mangers created for the public weal. That horse must be put out to pasture in the churchyard. Let the churches provide the green stuff to feed it!

We godless Americans are the ones who have to do it. We must act, and we must act forcefully and decisively.

We must expose the fallacies of religious thought both inside and outside of government.

We must prevent the relapse of our society into the Dark Ages.

We must set government once again upon the road of reason, the road of reality.

We must rebuild the wall of separation.

We must restore a semblance of sanity to government.

We must educate our representatives and our endangered nation.

We must not fail.

We dare not fail.

"Fundamentalism is becoming more extreme in the US."

Christian Fundamentalism Threatens America

Karen Armstrong

In the viewpoint that follows, Karen Armstrong examines the origins and growth of religious fundamentalism. Christian fundamentalism developed in the early twentieth century among American Protestants who were reacting against the liberalization of their churches, Armstrong explains. Over the years fundamentalists have grown more militant in their views, denouncing modernism and secularism as evil. Armstrong grants that American fundamentalists have not exhibited nearly as much violence as their Islamic counterparts. But many Christian fundamentalists believe in a violent future apocalypse, and some extremist factions harbor dangerously fascist and racist ideals. Armstrong, a former Catholic nun, is the author of *The Battle for God: Fundamentalism in Judaism, Christianity, and Islam.*

As you read, consider the following questions:
1. How does fundamentalism begin, in Armstrong's opinion?
2. According to the author, what percentage of the U.S. population is fundamentalist?
3. What early-twentieth-century event made American fundamentalists more "militantly literal" in their beliefs, according to Armstrong?

The US is the true home of religious extremism, which begins not as a crusade against outsiders, but as hatred of those of the same faith.

Fundamentalists of all faiths have convinced themselves that militant piety is the only way to save religion from annihilation in an increasingly secularised world. If we are to stand any chance of beating terrorists after the attacks on the United States, we must try to understand their motivation and fears.

A Reaction Against Modernity

This is not a centuries-old phenomenon. Fundamentalism actually began in the US early in the 20th century. Today, it is by no means confined to the Muslim world, but has erupted in every major faith as a reaction against rational, secular modernity. It did not become widespread in the Islamic world until a degree of modernisation had been achieved in the late 1960s, after secular solutions such as nationalism or socialism seemed to have failed.

Wherever a westernised secular state has established itself, a religious fundamentalist movement has developed in conscious rejection. Fundamentalists typically withdraw from mainstream society to create an enclave of pure faith, from the ultra-Orthodox Jewish communities in New York to the training camps of [terrorist] Osama Bin Laden. Surrounded by a world that they perceive as hostile, fundamentalists often plan a counter-offensive, resolved to drag God and religion from the sidelines in secular society and bring them back to centre stage.

In their sacred enclaves, fundamentalists often build a counterculture in conscious opposition. They overemphasise the traditional role of women, for example, because women's emancipation has been a hallmark of modernity. Often, these movements can be seen as the shadow-self of modern society, its distorted mirror image. As a result, many countries find that they are split into hostile camps: those who enjoy and value the ideals of secular humanism, and those who regard it with visceral fear and dread.

This is true of American fundamentalists as well as those in the Middle East. In the US today, about 8 per cent of the population can be described as fundamentalists, but they command widespread support from more conservative Christians in many denominations, as became evident during the rise of the Moral Majority in 1979.

The First Fundamentalists

It was American Protestants during the First World War who created the first fundamentalist movement, and who gave us the word "fundamentalist". Their aim was to respond to the liberalisation of their churches by returning to the "fundamentals" of the faith. The word has since been applied to Hindu, Buddhist, Muslim, Jewish, Sikh and even Confucian groups, which resent this Christian nomenclature, since they feel that they have quite different aims. Nevertheless, the term applies to movements that, for all their differences, bear a strong family resemblance.

As the primordial, archetypal fundamentalism, the American case reveals important aspects of this religious rebellion. First, it always begins as an assault on co-religionists, and is directed against foreigners and outsiders only at a later stage. American fundamentalism began as a battle for the control or the Protestant denominations, which were being controlled by more liberal Christians. It remains primarily an intra-Christian conflict.

Islamic fundamentalists initially directed their efforts against their own countrymen. Thus the movement that eventually gave birth to [the terrorist group] Hamas began as a revolt against the Palestine Liberation Organisation [PLO]; members were fighting for the Islamic soul of Palestine, and wanted to give the Palestinian struggle a Muslim, rather than a secularist, identity. Israel recognised this and, at first, funded Hamas to undermine the PLO; it was only after the outbreak of the 1987 intifada [uprising] that Hamas began to target Israelis.

Bin Laden's early offensive was directed against the regime of Saudi Arabia, which, he believed, had corrupted the Islamic ideal. He has also declared a jihad [holy war] against the secularist governments of Egypt, Syria and Jordan, and against the Shi'ite government of Iran. He now wishes to eliminate the American presence from the Middle

East because he sees it as the root cause of this widespread defection from the purity of Islam. The fundamentalist battle is not primarily directed against either Israel or the west per se; it is an intra-societal struggle.

A Response to Secularism

Fundamentalism always begins as a response to what is experienced as an assault by the liberal or secular world. The American fundamentalist movement began in earnest in 1917, after liberal Christians mounted an attack against their more conservative brethren, accusing them of undermining the war effort and of being in league with the Germans. The fundamentalists believed that the End of Days was nigh; they condemned democracy as mob rule, and saw the League of Nations as the abode of Antichrist. To this day, American fundamentalists are at best highly suspicious of democracy, and they regard the United Nations, the European Union and the World Council of Churches as satanic.

Fundamentalist Ire

In many cases, fundamentalists' ire is directed not only against business, political and artistic leaders who have shucked off the traditional constraints of religious, ethnic and tribal authority but also and even more strongly against religious leaders within their own faith who fundamentalists believe have adopted the same atheistic or indifferent attitude to religion.

"There is a sense in fundamentalisms that society experiences divorce and drugs and violence and various kinds of moral decadence, including the exploitation of women, precisely because the secular elites have advanced this agenda of the autonomous self, of the liberated individual who can be quite selective with regard to belief, practice, community ties," said [R. Scott] Appleby, a professor of history at the University of Notre Dame.

"It's not a trivial backlash," said Appleby, who noted that fundamentalists see the world dualistically and perceive themselves to be in a clash of good against evil.

Margot Patterson, *National Catholic Reporter*, May 7, 2004.

Those in the Middle East have also experienced modernity as evil and aggressive, and it's hardly surprising if they do not regard secularism as benign. When Ataturk began to secularise Turkey, he closed down all the madrasahs [Muslim schools] and forced the Sufi organisations underground.

In 1935, Shah Reza Pahlavi gave his soldiers orders to fire at unarmed demonstrators who were peacefully protesting against obligatory western dress in one of the holiest shrines in Iran: hundreds of Iranians died. Later, Iranian Shi'ite fundamentalism was born as a result of the aggressive secularism of Shah Muhammad Reza.

The type of Sunni fundamentalism loosely espoused by Osama Bin Laden was born in the concentration camps in which President Gamal Abdel Nasser had incarcerated Muslim activists, many of whom had done nothing more incriminating than handing out leaflets. Today, Muslims cite the bombing of Iraq, the death of thousands of Iraqi civilians after the Gulf war, and the destruction of Palestinian homes by American shells as the reason for this latest fundamentalist offensive against the US.

The American Experience

Americans have not resorted to the same degree of violence as Islamic fundamentalists because the attacks on them have been far less extreme. But they inveigh against the "secular humanism" of the federal government in language that often seems as paranoid as that used by their Muslim counterparts against America or Israel. In small-town America, people feel almost as "colonised" by the alien ethos of Yale, Harvard and Washington as do some of the inhabitants of Muslim countries.

The American experience also suggests that, when it is attacked, fundamentalism becomes more extreme. Before the Scopes trial of 1925, when Protestant fundamentalists tried to ban the teaching of evolution in schools, many fundamentalists had tended towards the left of the political spectrum. After the Scopes trial, when the fundamentalists were so ridiculed by the secular press that they seemed to suffer death by media, they swung to the far right and became much more militantly literal in their religious views.

Fundamentalism is becoming more extreme in the US, as well as in the Middle East. New American religious radicals now regard the Moral Majority as far too moderate; some are developing forms of Christian fascism. The most frightening of these movements is the network known as Christian Identity, which looks forward to the demise of the federal government. It is viciously racist, and it almost certainly influenced Timothy McVeigh, who bombed the federal building in Oklahoma in 1995.

Fears of extinction in Muslim countries centre on the military might of Israel and the Pentagon. When people believe they are fighting for survival, they will often lash out violently—but also in a nihilistic way. In their fear for the future of religion, fundamentalists of all hues distort the message of their scriptures, playing down the compassionate ethos of, for example, the Bible or the Koran. Bad religion, as we saw on 11 September [2001, when terrorists attacked the United States], can result in actions that are wholly evil.

Crackdowns and suppression will only make matters worse, because fundamentalism is rooted in a profound fear of annihilation. Every fundamentalist movement I have studied in Judaism, Christianity and Islam is convinced that secular society is determined to wipe out religion. In the US, extremists fear an insidious corruption of Godly America by books that promote a liberal or scientific ideal, or by the promotion of feminism, which they regard with horror.

Violent Theologies

While the vast majority of fundamentalists do not commit acts of terror, many cultivate violent theologies. American fundamentalists envisage an imminent End of Days, in which God will smash this wicked secular world and submerge its inhabitants in a tide of bloodshed. The collapse of the World Trade Centre [on September 11] bore a strong resemblance to this apocalyptic vision.

In Britain, we do not express our disquiet in religious terms, but the desire to belong to a clearly defined group, the sense of lost prestige, the pent-up rage and frustration that we see in our football [soccer] hooliganism show the same brew of emotions. This profound disaffection, wherever it occurs, indicates anxiety, anger and resentment that, as we have seen, no society can safely ignore.

"Fundamentalists are people with 'rigid doctrines'. . . . But what, you wonder, is a non-rigid doctrine?"

Christian Fundamentalism Does Not Threaten America

Report Newsmagazine

In the following viewpoint the editors of the Canadian *Report Newsmagazine* question the logic that equates American Christian evangelicalism with a dangerous form of fundamentalism. Since liberals tend to define both U.S. evangelicals and Islamic terrorists as fundamentalists, they often draw the erroneous conclusion that U.S. fundamentalists are violently dangerous, the authors point out. It is also wrong, in the authors' opinion, to bestow a negative connotation to the word *fundamentalism* since the term actually suggests a healthy capacity for commitment and clear-cut morality.

As you read, consider the following questions:

1. What is a false syllogism, according to the authors?
2. What is faulty about the argument that fundamentalists adhere to "rigid doctrines," in the authors' opinion?
3. In what way could Christ's call for belief be a call for "fundamentalism," in the authors' view?

While it's difficult to discover anything humorous about the events of September 11, [2001], one aspect of the aftermath is at least ironic, namely the strenuous efforts of our liberal element to blame the Christians for that catastrophe. In the following week, for example, one cantankerous Alberta [Canada] open-line host who constantly wars with God provided an especially striking example. It was religious extremists who did the deed, wasn't it? Christians are extremists too, aren't they? Christians shoot abortionists, don't they? So. . . .

So what? We're always left to supply the final thought: that whoever ultimately drove the planes into the World Trade Center and Pentagon and killed [thousands of] people, Christian attitudes were ultimately responsible. So why blame the Muslims? Why not blame the real culprits, the Christians?

We got the same message [in November 2001], in the *National Post* of all places, from Toronto columnist Robert Fulford in his approving review of a book by a lapsed Catholic and renegade nun. Her thesis, Mr. Fulford explained, is that four groups—Evangelicals in the United States, haredim Jews in Israel, Sunni Muslims in Egypt and Shiite Muslims in Iran—represent "a single world-wide phenomenon: religious fundamentalism."

Odd Reasoning

Thus president Anwar al-Sadat of Egypt was assassinated by a Muslim fundamentalist, prime minister Yitzhak Rabin of Israel was assassinated by a Jewish fundamentalist, and . . . and then what? Inconveniently, no head of state has been assassinated by a Christian Evangelical. But absence of evidence rarely impedes the free flow of liberal disquisition. Their reasoning runs as follows:

First: religious fundamentalists killed [thousands of] people in the U.S. on September 11, 2001. Second: Christian Evangelicals are religious fundamentalists. Third: therefore, Christian Evangelicals must be responsible for this.

Which, of course, parallels one of the classic false syllogisms, as in:

First: all dogs are animals. Second: my cat is an animal. Third: therefore, my cat is a dog.

Or you could look at it another way. Second World War soldiers fighting for the Nazi cause had a great deal in common with those fighting against it. Both were often cold, wet, exhausted and dirty, and preoccupied with many of the same things. Therefore (if we reason like Mr. Fulford), we must conclude that there was no significant difference between the Allied cause and the things the Nazis were fighting for. Their causes "resemble each other far more than most of them would care to admit," to use his terminology.

A Strange Expression

It is a very strange expression. Marxism is the ideas of Marx, and nationalism is the nation conceived as some sort of ideal identity. What is fundamentalism? What is this "fundament" promoted to an "ism"? It is slippery stuff whatever it is. It might, for example, refer to the irrational attachment some people have to a few basic ideas from which all conduct is said to follow. This does indeed seem to be one of its meanings. Or, it might refer to having any deeply held beliefs at all: ideas about dogmatism or bigotry: old stuff. But what fundamentalism actually means in the conventional wisdom of the moment is beliefs generated by some old text. In other words, "fundamentalism" is an all-purpose expression denigrating the peoples of the Book (as the Muslims call them). Anyone who takes the Bible (either Testament) or the Koran seriously falls under the terminological lash of terrorism-inducing fundamentalism.

Kenneth Minogue, *New Criterion*, June 2004.

We don't think so. To leap from the fact that soldiers on both sides think the same way, to the conclusion that the causes they're fighting for must also be the same, is absurd— an absurdity which Mr. Fulford takes two full columns of the *National Post* to expound.

What Is a Fundamentalist?

However, he does not so thoroughly expound something else. What exactly is a fundamentalist? You would think that in two columns he might include a couple words of definition. Well he does—precisely two words. Fundamentalists are people with "rigid doctrines," he tells us. But what, you wonder, is a non-rigid doctrine? Surely to the degree that it is not rigid, it is not a doctrine. It is a speculation. The whole point of a doctrine is to be rigid.

When Christ told Christians to "believe," he presumably meant to have faith in, to depend on, to consider true. We can recall no instance in which he was quietly adding, "but not rigidly." Indeed, the whole tenor of his directives seemed precisely to call for rigidity, for unreserved commitment. Therefore, by Mr. Fulford's own skimpy definition, Christ's cry for "belief" must have been a call for "fundamentalism." Which, to continue the Fulford thought process, must have been a call to do such things as murder [thousands of] civilians in downtown New York on a Tuesday morning.

What Mr. Fulford does not do, either here or anywhere else so far as I know, is address the following question: is it possible for human beings to know whether anything is good or true? I don't mean "true for them" or "good for them." I mean, is it possible for me, or for him, or for anybody, to actually know whether any statement is true for everybody, whether everybody agrees with it or not, or to know any form of human conduct to be good or bad for all of us, regardless of dissent?

If the answer is "No," that we cannot know anything in this "fundamental" way, then on what grounds can he criticize the behaviour of anyone else? When he condemns the horrors of Auschwitz [concentration camp], for example, he must merely be describing his own personal feelings about it. To suggest that what went on there was really wrong would imply a "fundamental" morality—which he says cannot be.

And if his answer is "Yes," that we can indeed know such things, then doesn't that make him a "fundamentalist" too, right in there with the Taliban and the Southern Baptists? Maybe one day he will favour us with a column on this question.

"We are being cudgeled toward theocracy."

Politicians' Promotion of Religion Is Unacceptable

Ronnie Dugger

The United States may be degenerating into a theocracy, as evidenced by what has occurred during the presidency of George W. Bush, argues Ronnie Dugger in the following viewpoint. Bush has given an unprecedented level of political support to religious institutions by funneling tax dollars to churches, Dugger points out. In addition, Bush has used federal funds to promote marriage among the poor and has opposed the legalization of gay marriage. This political endorsement of a selective religious agenda is unacceptable and should be resisted by all who value constitutional freedoms, Dugger maintains. Dugger is a writer and a cofounder of the Alliance for Democracy.

As you read, consider the following questions:

1. In Dugger's opinion, what was the real reason behind George W. Bush's support for the federal funding of religious social-service programs?
2. What question concerning marriage and divorce does Dugger suggest that reporters ask Bush?
3. Why did a public school social studies teacher in Maine sue his school district, according to the author?

Ronnie Dugger, "It's Time for an American Offensive Against Theocracy," *Free Inquiry*, vol. 24, April/May 2004, p. 16. Copyright © 2004 by Council for Democratic and Secular Humanism, Inc. Reproduced by permission.

This is the right historical moment to launch a national offensive against the degeneration of the United States into a theocracy. Pressures to subordinate democratic pluralism to fundamentalist domination have converged into the presidency of George W. Bush.

Bush identifies himself as a born-again Christian and continues to violate the Constitution by ladling out government funds to churches of his administration's choice. In January [2004], for the first time, Congress appropriated our tax dollars to re-direct public school students into religious schools, beginning in the District of Columbia. Bush communicates to writers such as Carl Woodward his belief that he is God's agent as he wages worldwide war in his self-declared mission to end evil on Earth. If all this keeps up without decisive resistance, we might as well resign ourselves to the transformation of the White House into a fortified cathedral.

Proselytizing and Politics

For too long we have tolerated the moral cowardice of those congressional politicians who added "under God" to the Pledge of Allegiance. Where does this language leave the patriotism of youngsters of secular disposition or belief who are required to rise in the classrooms of the nation and recite what they do not believe? And why not "under Allah"? Why not "under Yahweh"?

Why not "under God, Jehovah, Allah, Buddha, Gandhi, or Wicca?" Why not? Because the Constitution that secured the freedom of Americans from religious domination in England and the Colonies stipulates that Congress shall make no law that establishes religion.

[Since 2001] Bush, acting by unconstitutional executive order, has given tens of millions of our tax money to churches of the government's choice for the social-service programs through which they dispense charity and recruit new members. Religious proselytizing, spooned in along with the charity, is by no means prohibited.

Bush calls this "unleashing the compassion of America's religious institutions." Who, pray, is "leashing" the Catholic Church, or the Episcopalian, the Baptist—or Judaism or Islam—by not giving them federal tax money? If we choose to support religious institutions, the way we do it legally is by giving them money directly, not by establishing them with funds from the federal government. What Bush is actually doing is using everyone's tax money to promote the recruitment programs of the evangelical Christian denominations that he regards as his political base and to seek to seduce influential Black ministers to weaken opposition among Black voters to his election [in 2004].

In his State of the Union speech in January [2004], Bush declared: "By executive order, I have opened billions of dollars in grant money to competition that includes faith-based charities. Tonight, I ask you to codify this into law." That is, he is now asking Congress to legalize and multiply his gifts of federal tax money to religious institutions for them to dispense as charity and to get new members. Congress can do this legally only if it repeals the establishment clause or lets Bush stack the Supreme Court with a clear majority for [fundamentalists] Jerry Falwell and Pat Robertson.

By the same presidential fiat, Bush has exempted favored churches from the national laws against discrimination in employment, as if he were a king whom we permitted to excuse his chosen allies from the laws the rest of us must obey.

Toward Religious Dictatorship

Both consensual sex and marriage among adults are strictly the business of the people directly concerned. The state's only legitimate interest in either subject is the protection and education of children. Yet Bush also proposed in January [2004] that we spend $1.5 billion in federal funds to promote marriage, especially among the poor. He's worried about lust and degeneracy not among the well-to-do but in the slums of the poor. He is against raising the minimum wage or strengthening labor unions or job security or subsidizing child care or taking any of the other real steps that would improve the lives of the poor. Instead, he wants Uncle Sam butting into their personal lives, teaching them to marry and not to divorce— one more program toward turning the United States into a religious dictatorship over personal matters of the sort that historically has been exercised by, for example, the Catholic Church, certain puritanical Protestant sects, and Islam.

Like a plaintiff lawyer who accidentally lets his client's credibility become an issue in a trial, Bush has opened himself to hard questions in this area by threatening, in his [2004] State of the Union, to use "the constitutional process" to block "activist judges" such as those in the 4-3 majority on the Supreme Judicial Court in Massachusetts who ruled that gays must be allowed to marry. It is past time for the reporters in the White House press corps to stop giving Bush a free ride with his ambiguous and hypocritical pieties. Any good reporter with a dash of imagination and a gram of gumption can think up good questions for him here.

Conrad. © 1997 by Tribune Media Services. Reproduced by permission.

For example: half of the marriages in the United States end in divorce. Bush has said that the philosopher who most inspired him is Jesus Christ. Jesus told his disciples, "Whoever divorces his wife and marries another, commits adultery against her; and if she divorces her husband and marries another, she commits adultery" (Mark 10:9–12). The question: "Mr. President, do you agree with Jesus that remarriage is adultery, and if so would you favor a constitutional amendment to prohibit divorce?" Let the born-again president answer yes or no before the entire American people.

Marriage Counseling?

A rift on the Internet suggested that what Bush and his "base" really want to do is codify marriage on biblical principles. This sent me back to re-reading the Old as well as the New Testament. If brothers live together and one is married but dies without a son, the surviving brother is expected to marry his brother's widow. If he refuses, in the presence of her elders she is to pull his sandal off his foot and spit in his face (Deut. 25:5–10). A constitutional amendment requiring marriage on biblical principles would give fathers the right to choose the husbands for their daughters (Gen. 29:17–28). The supreme male leaders, however, could take as many wives and concubines as they want (King Solomon loved many foreign women and had seven hundred wives and three hundred concubines; Rehoboam, king of the cities of Judah, had eighteen wives, sixty concubines, twenty-eight sons, and sixty daughters, but loved the daughter of Absalom above all of them [Kings 11:3, 2 Chron. 11:21]). If two men are fighting and the wife of one of them seizes the private parts of the other one, "then you shall cut off her hand" (Deut. 25:11–12). A new wife who is discovered not to be a virgin is to be stoned to death at "the door of her father's house" (Deut. 22:13–21). If it's biblical marriage Bush has in view for us, perhaps he should be devoting the whole federal budget to marriage counseling.

The distance between American Catholics' personal decisions and Catholic doctrines continues to widen. [In June 2003], the Vatican said that votes by elected legislators to legalize gay marriage are "gravely immoral." Although polls have shown that about half of Catholics do not oppose gay marriage, the four Catholic bishops of Massachusetts are sending out talking points for priests in the pulpits and a million brochures into Catholic households, explicitly lobbying in favor of a state constitutional amendment to prohibit it. This is the specter of men who have never been married—either to women or to men—using their religious high-dudgeon to tell the rest of us what we can and cannot do in our private lives: it is the specter of theocracy replacing democracy. *Boston Globe* columnist Eileen McNamara wrote, in the context of the Church leaders' systematic protection of pedophile priests from exposure and the law, that the bishops "are in urgent need of remedial education about human sexuality" and "should be asking questions, not issuing directives."

Christian Theocracy?

To be sure President Bush opposes Islamic theocracy for Iraq, but does he oppose Christian theocracy for the United States? Let some reporter ask him outright whether he believes in the separation of church and state. Or pick any test case at hand. In Presque Isle, Maine, a public school social-studies teacher sued his school district, complaining that "a small group of fundamentalist Christian individuals" won the adoption of a curriculum which prohibits him from teaching his students about any religion but Christianity and any civilization but Christian ones. Is that OK with the president? Is it OK with Americans? Since, in fundamentalist redoubts throughout the country, now nationally, we are being cudgeled toward theocracy, let's put up one ferocious fight for our freedoms of and from religion.

| *"For political leaders to use biblical categories to describe their policies is hardly inappropriate."*

Politicians' Promotion of Religion Is Acceptable

Christianity Today

Many commentators have recently criticized religious convictions expressed by politicians in public dialogue. Specifically, many are concerned that President George W. Bush has overstepped his bounds by using religious language to discuss his policies. In the following viewpoint the editors of *Christianity Today* contend that Bush's invocation of religion is neither irrational, nor fanatical, nor unusual for American presidents. Particularly during the difficulties America is currently facing, it is beneficial to have a national leader who uses moral language and who can make moral judgments, the authors assert. Observers should be less concerned about the fact that a politician has religious views and focus more on whether the policies arising from those views are effective. *Christianity Today* is a monthly magazine of evangelical Christian opinion.

As you read, consider the following questions:

1. How do the authors respond to the charge that George W. Bush's religious views might alienate those of other faiths?
2. Why do Christians have a clear understanding of human fallibility, in the authors' opinion?
3. What other presidents used religious language in the public square, according to the authors?

Christianity Today, "Free Speech for Politicians: God-Talk in the Public Square Is Healthy," vol. 47, May 2003. Copyright © 2003 by Christianity Today, Inc. Reproduced by permission.

"**G**od has ordered you to cut their throats." Reading editorials in the last few months [of early 2003], you would think that line comes straight from President George W. Bush. In fact, this bellicose statement came from [Iraqi leader] Saddam Hussein in the first week of the Iraq War. Yet it is President George W. Bush who alarms pundits because he often uses religious language to discuss his policies.

Georgie Anne Geyer, writing in the *Chicago Tribune* of March 7 [2003], argued that the President's intention to invade Iraq "is based primarily on religious obsession and visions of personal grandiosity." In the *Times* (London) of March 1 [2003], Stephen Plant wrote, "Bush's supporters have inherited the idea of manifest destiny. For them war on Iraq is not about oil, it is America's next date with salvation."

Typical Complaints

Three typical complaints can be dismissed quickly.

• *Religion and rationality.* On a recent McLaughlin Group broadcast, Eleanor Cliff said she worried that Bush's "religiosity" doesn't allow "logical, rational thought," and Princeton University religion professor Elaine Pagels said, "Religious language . . . bypasses the brain and goes straight to the gut." It surprises us that, with Christianity's impressive intellectual tradition (consider Augustine and Aquinas), educated people are still saying such things. If one were mean-spirited, one might argue that secularism doesn't allow for logical, rational thought about religion.

• *Religion and debate.* "When you use religious language you stifle debate," said C. Welton Gaddy, a Baptist pastor and president of the Interfaith Alliance, and an op-ed piece in the *New York Times* repeated the charge. Apparently such commentators have never seen the sparks fly at a denominational meeting or a theological society. And they are apparently not reading many newspapers, for religious language seems to be having the opposite effect. That strikes us as a good thing in a democracy.

• *Religion and alienating other faiths.* "When he speaks in these terms," said Gaddy, "he leaves out whole segments of America." To be sure, a politician's language can needlessly alienate important constituencies, but in a pluralistic society, one hopes political leaders from various religious perspectives will use language that help us see their own deeper commitments. We don't have to agree with them, but we will be a smaller society if we tell everyone to leave their deepest convictions behind when they speak in the public square.

Can We Know God's Will?

One concern does deserve more comment. As historian Martin Marty put it in a March 10 [2003], *Newsweek* essay, many are fretting about Bush's "evident conviction that he's doing God's will." For some, this worry is grounded in a nihilism that assumes we are alone in history and cannot discern God's ways for the world.

Reflecting Religious Diversity

The University of Akron's [John] Green finds [George W. Bush's] remarks—even his contention that God is on America's side—not unusual or inappropriate. "Most of his religious utterances are well within the bounds of American political discourse," Green says. "When you read the speeches of Washington, Lincoln or FDR, there is the notion that divine providence is with us and is supporting our cause."

Emory University's [Patrick] Allitt agrees. "I don't think you can say that he's out of the norm in the modern era of American politics," he says, "because even though he invokes God, he never says anything that is too religiously explicit. For instance, he doesn't say that 'America is a Christian republic,' which is something politicians used to say frequently in the 19th century."

Supporters also dismiss the argument that the president's remarks alienate people of other faiths or nonbelievers. Indeed, they say, Bush's remarks very much reflect the religious diversity of the country and strive not to exclude people of other faiths. "You'll notice that he will say 'church, synagogue and mosque,' which means he's trying to be even-handed," Allitt says.

David Masci, *CQ Researcher*, July 30, 2004.

Marty would agree, we think, that humans can discern God's will in broad outline—God is against oppression and for liberty, for example—and that in prayer we can often discern his leading about specific steps to accomplish that will.

Granted, our sense of that leading can be mistaken, but it is the Christian's duty to discern God's will and act on faith, relying always on God's mercy.

Some worry that talk about God's will is a symptom of megalomania, a mad certitude that brooks no dissent. This diagnosis fits Hussein's rhetoric, but it is difficult to see how Bush fits this description. As E.J. Dionne, hardly a champion of Bush's policies, put it in a February [2003] *New York Post* column: "Can we please stop pretending that Bush's regular invocations of the Almighty make him some sort of strange religious fanatic? In this, he is much more typically presidential than he's painted, especially by our friends abroad."

The Complexity of Religious Language

Many critics don't understand the complexity of religious and specifically Judeo-Christian language. Through religious language, as Fuller Theological Seminary President Richard Mouw recently put it, Bush "has reintroduced into the culture the language of morality and moral distinctions." Even a critic like Pagels recognizes this value: "We need moral language to better understand horrific acts, such as the terror attacks of [September 11, 2001]."

Yet that same language points beyond the world to the source of morality, a Creator who, according to the biblical tradition, stands above all human aspirations and opinions. In making religious/moral judgments, the speaker yields to a greater authority. In the Christian tradition, this tends to instill a clear perception of human fallibility. And thus Bush, in his [2003] State of the Union address, not only outlined his moral vision in foreign affairs but acknowledged that "we do not claim to know all the ways of Providence, yet we can trust in them, placing our confidence in the loving God behind all of life, and all of history."

This is not to defend all the President's speeches, or to pretend that some previous American forays into religiously tinged policies (some of those based on "manifest destiny," for instance) were not disasters. It is only to suggest that for political leaders to use biblical categories to describe their policies is hardly inappropriate. Bush is certainly not the first President to do so—though this tradition was only recently revived. Many have forgotten the nation's surprise when Bill Clinton began inserting religious allusions into his remarks.

Let's move from wringing our hands that Bush or any politician has a religious worldview, and stick to debating whether the specific policies that emerge from that worldview actually bring peace and justice to the world.

*"There are fantastic programs all
throughout the country . . . all based upon
faith, all changing lives, all making
American life better."*

Faith-Based Social Programs Benefit America

George W. Bush

In the following viewpoint George W. Bush maintains that faith-based social programs benefit needy Americans and should therefore receive federal funding. Faith-based services are providing after-school programs, building housing projects, creating job-training programs for ex-convicts, and mentoring at-risk children, Bush points out. Enlisting help from faith communities is especially effective because it delivers hope and inspiration as it saves lives, he argues. Bush is the forty-third president of the United States. This viewpoint is excerpted from a speech he delivered before a group of urban leaders in Washington, D.C., on July 18, 2003.

As you read, consider the following questions:
1. How does Bush define "social entrepreneurs"?
2. What is governmental "faith-based discrimination," in Bush's opinion?
3. What is the Capital Compassion Fund, according to the author?

George W. Bush, "Remarks to Urban Leaders: Week Ending July 18, 2003," *Weekly Compilation of Presidential Documents*, vol. 39, p. 920.

I thank you all for coming. I'm joined by some pretty distinguished company up here. I want to thank my friends, the social entrepreneurs of America, for standing up here today. . . .

Let's talk about the values that make our country unique and different. We love freedom here in America. We believe freedom is God's gift to every single individual, and we believe in the worth of each individual. We believe in human dignity, and we believe where we find hopelessness and suffering, we shall not turn our back. That's what we believe.

The American Dream Is for Everybody

And there are—in this land of plenty, there are people who hurt, people who wonder whether or not the American experience, what they call the American Dream, is meant for them. And I believe the American Dream is meant for everybody. And when we find there's doubt, we've got to bring light and hope, and so that's what we're here to talk about today. And the men up here represent a representative sample of what we call the faith community in America, people who first and foremost have been called because of a calling much higher than government.

I say "social entrepreneurs" because, in many of our faith institutions, we find people who are willing to reach out in the neighborhood in which they exist to help those who hurt and those who are in need. They're willing to take a new tack, a tack based upon faith, to heal hearts and provide hope and provide inspiration, so that the American Dream is available in every corner in America. And where we find those programs which are effective, society ought to support those programs.

Funding Effective Programs

What I'm saying is, we ought not to fear faith. We ought not to discriminate against faith-based programs. We ought to welcome what I call neighborhood healers in the compassionate delivery of help so that people can experience the greatness of our country.

Of course, that then leads to the question of public money, taxpayers' money. My attitude is, taxpayers' money should and must fund effective programs, effective faith-based programs, so long as those services go to anybody in need. We ought to focus on—we ought to ask the question in our society, "Is the faith-based program working," not focus on the fact that it's a faith-based program.

The Government, as it gives support, as it provides help to the faith-based program and in return asks for help for solving social problems, as it does that, it should never discriminate. It should never cause the faith-based program to lose its character or to compromise the mission. That's the basic principles of the Faith-Based Initiative which you've heard a lot about. Really what we're doing is, we're signing up the armies of compassion which already exist and saying, "What can we do to help you fulfill your calling and your mission?" That's really what we're doing.

I signed an Executive order banning discrimination against faith-based charities by Federal agencies. We waited for Congress to act. They couldn't act on the issue. So I just went ahead and signed an Executive order which . . . says the Federal agencies will not discriminate against faith-based programs. They ought to welcome the armies of compassion as opposed to turning them away. . . .

Look, I fully understand the issue, the frustration some face. And it's a frustration based upon a long practice here at the Federal level, and that is, there's no place for faith-based programs and trying to help people in need. And therefore, we'll discriminate, shove out of the way, not deal with, make it hard for, create barriers to entry. And my administration is absolutely committed to reducing those barriers to entry. And we've created these offices whose sole function it is to, one, recognize the power of faith and, two, recognize there are fantastic programs all throughout the country on a variety of subjects, all based upon faith, all changing lives, all making American life better, and therefore, folks would be enlisted in making sure the American Dream extends throughout our society.

Faith-Based Discrimination

And let me give you some examples. . . . People [ask] "What do you mean by faith-based discrimination?" Well, in Seattle, there was an earthquake, and the Federal Emergency Management Agency [FEMA] gave disaster relief funds to schools but denied them to the Seattle Hebrew Academy. In other words, schools—public schools got the funds from FEMA, but not a religious school. And so, we've changed that rule. That's the kind of discrimination that I—that may make some sense to people who are not exactly sure what I'm talking about.

Another interesting example is, in Boston, the Old North Church, the famous historic landmark, needed preservation funds; yet it was denied Federal help because it was a church. And that's not right. That's not right. It makes no sense, and therefore, we're changing those kinds of rules.

And we're also making sure that Federal monies are available. It's one thing to talk about a Faith-Based Initiative, but there needs to be money in the system available for the faith-based programs in order for—to make it work. And that's money that's coming out of these agencies already. I mean, there's—we spend a lot of money here in Washington, and that—monies ought to be accessible to effective faith-based programs which heal people from all walks of life. It's—money is not going to proselytize; money is going to save lives.

What Works

And let me give you some examples of what is working today, maybe examples that you already have heard about, particularly when you go to the White House conferences as we try to describe how to access the system.

In Columbus, Ohio, St. Stephen's Community House—faith-based program—is using a—nearly $1 million from the Department of Education to expand its after-school program. There's kind of an interesting use of education dollars that will help faith-based programs fulfill their mission.

The Frederick Douglass Community Development Corporation, started by the Memorial AME Zion Church in Rochester, New York, has received more than $5 million from HUD [Housing and Urban Development] to build low-income houses for seniors. The AME Church decided to do something about the housing issue, as far as the seniors go in their congregation, and accessed Federal money and put together a housing project. Now a lot of people . . . when they think about the AME Church or any church for that matter, they don't think housing. Except I know some social entrepreneurs from my State . . . who have used their facilities, their skills to go ahead and to build homes.

Religion and Crime

A four-year longitudinal, stratified, random-sample study of high school students in the Rocky Mountain region, published in 1975, demonstrated that religious involvement significantly decreased drug use, delinquency, and premarital sex, and also increased self-control. A 1989 study of midwestern high school students replicated these findings. Similarly, young religious adults in Canada were found in a 1979 study to be less likely to use or sell narcotics, to gamble, or to destroy property.

What is true for youth is also true for adults. Religious behavior, as opposed to mere attitude or affiliation, is associated with reduced crime.

Patrick Fagan, *Heritage Foundation Backgrounder No. 1064*, January 25, 1996.

The Operation New Hope and City Center Ministries in Jacksonville, Florida, and the Exodus Transitional Community in East Harlem went to the Department of Labor, and they received labor funds for job training programs for ex-offenders. A person gets out of prison, checks in at the church, and the church says, "Wait, we want to help you get back into society; not only will there be some lessons to be learned, but also, here's some training money. Here's a training course." So it's a practical application of taxpayers' money to meet societal needs. And one of the greatest societal needs is [that] we have is to make sure our—you know, a guy who's spent time in the pen not only receives spiritual guidance and love, but spiritual guidance and love can only go so far. And it's also helpful to have him be trained in a job which exists. In other words, there's practical application of taxpayers' money that we want to get into the hands of our faith-based organizations all throughout our society.

People say, "Well, we're already doing that." Now, what's happening is that the same programs are being funded over and over and over again. In other words, there's kind of a rut.

And that doesn't encourage the entrepreneurial spirit that we're interested in. . . .

We've got an office dedicated, by the way, to the Faith-Based Initiative. And we've started White House conferences to explain to people how the process works. . . .

Enlisting the Faith Community

We've got to do a better job of making sure that we explain what we mean by the Faith-Based Initiative. I understand that. It requires education. People can read everything they want into it. When they hear "Faith-Based Initiative," they— that all of a sudden opens everybody's imagination in the world to vast possibilities, some which exist and some which don't.

And so therefore we're reaching out to explain to people the practical applications. The Compassion—Capital Compassion Fund, which Congress has funded—I've asked for $100 million; they gave it 30 million and 35 million over the last 2 years—but that money goes to help smaller charities learn how to fill out grants, learn what it means to access Federal monies.

It's one thing for people, however, to learn how to fill out a grant. It's another thing to have the grant fall on deaf ears. So we're also changing habits here in Washington, DC. And that's what . . . these departments are all designed to do, to facilitate, to make it easier for people to access, to make sure that we really do tap the heart and soul of our country.

[The Reverend] Tony Evans first kind of woke me up to this. We were in Greenville, Texas, together, and he said, "The best welfare programs already exist on the street corners of inner-city Dallas," in this case. "They're open 24 hours a day." They've got a fantastic guidebook, been around a long time. "The motto of the work force is clear: Love your neighbor." And it dawned on me how true he is. There's no need to reinvent. We've got it in place. And so therefore, when I lay out an initiative that talks about saving the lives of drug offenders, really what I'm saying is, is that I understand that when you change a person's heart, you can change their habits. So let's enlist it, the faith community, on the goal of saving people's lives who happen to be hooked on drugs.

Six hundred million dollars over 3 years—I would hope that the faith community gets very much involved when Congress funds this. And by the way, part of this mission is for me to remind Congress they need to fund it. But once funded, it's very important for the faith community to be involved. The 10-step program is a faith initiative, when you really think about the—how it works. And I know many of you who run churches and synagogues and mosques in America are worried about addiction in your neighborhoods. And we want to help because we believe—we know—that some of the most effective programs are those that work when a heart is changed.

Mentoring Initiatives

I've also laid out a mentoring initiative. I would love to have every child who has a mother or dad in prison to have a mentor. The most vulnerable of our population are those who may have a mom or a dad incarcerated. And they need love. They need a lot of love. And the best way to provide love is to find somebody who's willing to love them through a mentoring program.

I went to the Amachi program in Philadelphia—perhaps you all know about it—out of the Bright Hope Baptist Church, saw the program that works. There's a lot of initiatives around from the faith-based program that track the child who needs to be mentored. And the best place to find mentors, of course, is you can find them every Sunday. But we need help to make sure the program works. . . .

My point is, we've got some Federal initiatives, job training, education, addiction. We've got a housing initiative here, by the way, that I'm deeply concerned about, what they call a minority gap in America. Too many—relative to the Anglo community, too many minorities don't own their own homes. I believe in an ownership society. I know when somebody owns their home, they've got such a fantastic stake in the future.

The faith community can help in homeownership. The Federal Government's got to help a lot here. We've got to make sure there is more affordable homes. We've got to provide tax incentives for people to build homes in inner cities. We've got to have downpayment help. And we've got to make sure that the contracts—I can understand somebody, a first-time homebuyer, getting a little nervous when they pull up the contract and the print's about that big, and nobody understands what's in the print. And a lot of people don't want to sign something they're not sure what it's about. And so we've got education programs through our housing institutions to teach people what it means to buy a home and how to help them access the downpayment help and also to make sure the contracts are clear and understandable.

Helping People

This is a mission at home to help people. And you know, Government can help. I like to say, Government can pass out money, but it cannot put hope in people's hearts or purpose in people's lives. And that's why it's vital for our country to count on those who can put hope in people's hearts and a sense of purpose in people's lives, and that's our faith community.

You know, we will accomplish a lot here at home if we use all the resources available to our communities. And I will tell—continue to tell the American people, one of the great untapped resources for Government is to work side by side with the faith community. And I want to thank you all for . . . hearing the call.

"There is no evidence that faith-based organizations work better than their secular counterparts; and, in some cases, they are actually less effective."

Faith-Based Social Programs Are Not as Effective as Secular Programs

Amy Sullivan

In the year 2001 President George W. Bush launched a "faith-based initiative" that allowed religious organizations to obtain government grants to provide social services. Bush and his supporters have long maintained that religious groups achieve better results than nonreligious service providers do. In the viewpoint that follows, Amy Sullivan disagrees, contending that no studies have shown that faith-based groups are more successful than secular organizations in addressing social problems. Furthermore, Sullivan points out, well-established secular organizations now receive less funding because they must compete with unproven—and often less-effective—religious groups for grants. The result is that fewer people receive the assistance they need. Sullivan is an editor for the *Washington Monthly*.

As you read, consider the following questions:

1. According to Sullivan, what did a Ford Foundation study conclude about faith-based job training programs?
2. What argument is made in the Bush administration's report "Unlevel Playing Field," according to the author?

Amy Sullivan, "Faith Without Works: After Four Years, the President's Faith-Based Policies Have Proven to Be Neither Compassionate nor Conservative," *Washington Monthly*, vol. 36, October 2004, pp. 30–33. Copyright © 2004 by Washington Monthly Publishing LLC, 733 15th St. NW, Suite 520, Washington, DC 20005. (202) 393-5155. Web site: www.washingtonmonthly.com. Reproduced by permission.

When George W. Bush first hit the national political scene in the crowded field for the 2000 Republican nomination, what made him different, what made even liberal Americans take a second look, was his declaration that he was a "compassionate conservative." Unlike the flinty old conservatives of the past, Bush explained, a compassionate conservative would not be afraid to harness the power of government to minister to the unfortunate. But unlike traditional liberal Democrats, who relied on fumbling government bureaucracies, a compassionate conservative would empower and fund the charitable sector, particularly religious groups, to help those in need.

A Faith-Based Initiative

This breakthrough political slogan was embodied by a "faith-based initiative" that Bush talked about incessantly on the campaign trail and rolled out within the first month of taking over the White House. And Bush's image as a different kind of Republican was only reinforced by the tableau of black pastors, conservative evangelical leaders, and liberal crusaders for social justice who gathered around him as he introduced his faith-based domestic policy. The first part of the initiative sought to make it easier for religious organizations to get government grants to provide social services. Trumpeting the success of faith-based groups in Texas that ran drug rehabilitation and prison counseling programs, Bush argued that religious organizations could outperform their secular equivalents and so should be allowed to compete for the same government funds. The policy's second aspect was a proposed tax break to make it worthwhile for individuals to contribute more of their money to charities. By allowing non-itemizers (70 percent of taxpayers) to deduct their charitable contributions, the proposal could infuse as much as $80 billion into the charitable sector. Together, the two ideas embraced classic conservative principles honoring the unique ability of religious organizations to help those in need, and empowering individuals in the civil sector instead of government.

Four years later, Bush's compassionate conservatism has turned out to be neither compassionate nor conservative. The policy of funding the work of faith-based organizations has, in the face of slashed social service budgets, devolved into a small pork-barrel program that offers token grants to . . . religious constituencies. . . . while making almost no effort to monitor their effectiveness. Meanwhile, the plan to extend tax credits for charitable giving has gone nowhere, despite the . . . enormous tax cut packages Bush has signed. Like any number of this administration's policies, the faith-based initiative has been so ill-considered, so utterly sacrificed to political expediency, and carried out with so little regard for the problems it was supposed to solve, that it bears only the faintest resemblance to the political philosophy it was supposed to embody. The history of the faith-based initiative tells us little about what could have been a truly innovative social policy, but speaks volumes about the cynical politics of the Bush administration.

Blind Faith

From the very beginning, Bush has argued that faith-based groups should be judged on their results, and he insists that they do work better. The difference, he contends, is that they do more than simply minister to physical needs. On the campaign trail in the summer of 2000, Bush told audiences that religious organizations succeed where others fail "because they change hearts, they convince a person to turn their life over to Christ." Whenever "my administration sees a responsibility to help people," he promised, "we will look first to faith-based organizations that have shown their ability to save and change lives." Bush had little empirical evidence to back up the claim that religious organizations were more effective. But he relentlessly talked of two seemingly-promising programs that the Texas state government had supported while he was governor. One was Teen Challenge, a drug rehabilitation program that claimed an astonishing 86 percent success rate. The other was InnerChange, a counseling program for prisoners that boasted impressively low levels of recidivism among its graduates. Certain critics raised questions about the reliability of the studies that produced these figures. But Bush kept repeating the claims, and most of the press corps passed them along uncritically.

Once in office, Bush wasted no time setting up a new bureaucratic structure to cater specifically to the needs of faith-based groups. He created a White House Office of Faith-Based and Community Initiatives and appointed political scientist John DiIulio (a Democrat) to run it before his first week was out; soon after, the White House sent proposed legislation to Congress that would expand federal grant eligibility to religious groups. But the proposal came loaded with a number of controversial provisions, including giving religious contractors the right not to hire employees of a different faith, a clear violation of federal anti-discrimination statutes. When the legislation, which DiIulio himself described as "an absolute political non-starter," went nowhere, Bush didn't bat an eye. He simply pulled out his pen and implemented his idea via a series of executive orders instead.

Casting Doubt on Faith-Based Efforts

Although advocates of the "charitable-choice" programs have often argued that religiously motivated charities are more effective at providing social services than their governmental or secular counterparts, [one] study's researchers concluded otherwise. Among other results, the Charitable Choice Research Project found:

• Religious organizations operating job-training programs placed 31 percent of their clients in full-time employment, while secular job-training organizations place 53 percent of their clients.

• Those placed in jobs from secular job-training programs were more likely to have health benefits and to work more hours than were graduates of religious programs.

• "Relatively few" new religious groups in the states studied have begun accepting government money to perform social services.

Christian Century, November 29, 2003.

Critics worried that faith-based groups would be unduly privileged in the newly expanded grant-making world. For them, Bush had one word: results, results, results. In an interview with the religious Web site Beliefnet, he was asked whether he would support government money going to a Muslim group that taught prisoners the Koran. "The question I'd be asking," Bush replied, "is what are the recidivism rates? Is it working? I wouldn't object at all if the program worked." Four more times in the interview, Bush mentioned "results," noting that instead of promoting religion, "I'm promoting lower recidivism rates, and we will measure to make sure that's the case."

This rhetoric matched the administration's focus in other policy areas—like education—on accountability. Conservatives traditionally criticize government programs for throwing good money after bad, rewarding those who have not proven themselves effective with hard numbers like higher test scores, lower poverty rates, or reduced recidivism. Mel Martinez, Secretary of Housing and Urban Development [HUD], echoed the results-oriented sentiment in December 2002, telling an audience that "faith-based organizations should be judged on one central question: Do they work?" Conservatives thought they already knew the answer. "The fact is, we don't just suspect that faith-based programs work best," said Tucker Carlson on *Crossfire*, "we know it."

What Studies Show

Actually, we knew no such thing. But now we've had four years to measure results and reach a conclusion. Unfortunately, in the midst of all of the instructions included in the various executive orders, it turns out that the Bush administration forgot to require evaluation of organizations that receive government grants. According to a study released by the Pew-funded Roundtable on Religion and Social Welfare Policy in August 2004, "while more elaborate scientific studies are underway, the White House has relied on largely anecdotal evidence to support the view that faith-based approaches produce better long-term results." The accountability president has chosen not to direct any money toward figuring out whether faith-based approaches really work.

So it's a good thing that some academics and private organizations have picked up the slack. In the last few years, a few studies have looked at both faith-based and secular social service providers, and they have particularly tried to replicate the incredible results boasted by the model Texas programs. The verdict? There is no evidence that faith-based organizations work better than their secular counterparts; and, in some cases, they are actually less effective. In one study funded by the Ford Foundation, investigators found that faith-based job training programs placed only 31 percent of their clients in full-time employment while the number for secular organizations was 53 percent. And Teen Challenge's much ballyhooed 86 percent rehabilitation rate falls apart under examination—the number doesn't include those who dropped out of Teen Challenge and relies on a disturbingly small sample of those graduates who self-reported whether they had remained sober, significantly tilting the results.

It will take several more years to rigorously scrutinize the relative abilities of faith-based and secular organizations to provide effective social services, so it is impossible to know whether these initial findings are true across the board. And maybe in a perfect world it would be worth testing Bush's hunch and giving faith-based groups access to funds in the effort to alleviate poverty and other social problems. The problem is that, under the Bush administration, the overall pot of money for social services has shrunk considerably. This means that well-established organizations that have provided services for decades are now competing with—and, in some cases, being displaced by—unproven, often less-successful groups, inflicting a double whammy upon the people who really need the help.

The Chosen Ones

The fact that there is no proof that faith-based programs are more effective has not stopped the president from claiming that they are. But, as he has in other areas—take the ever-changing rationale for invading Iraq—Bush simply shifts his emphasis when one argument begins to lose luster. These days, he is most likely to promote the faith-based initiative by contending that religious groups have been discriminated against and merely deserve the same chances that everyone else has. To lay the groundwork for this point, the administration published a report in the summer of 2001 assessing the "barriers" to government cooperation with religious groups. Titled "Unlevel Playing Field," this audit of federal agencies argued that faith-based organizations have been unfairly locked out of participation in government programs simply because of their religious nature.

And, in fact, federal policy has not always been blind to religious character. This is often for good reason—the Constitution prohibits government promotion of religion—but it sometimes seems arbitrary. In 2001, for example, after an earthquake struck Seattle, a number of groups applied for FEMA [Federal Emergency Management Agency] funds to rebuild structures, particularly historic buildings in the downtown district. When members of a synagogue applied for money, however, they were initially turned down because FEMA regulations didn't allow government funds to go toward the construction of houses of worship. After the group lodged a complaint, the rules were changed to make religious communities eligible for aid to rebuild their damaged structures. So the concern isn't entirely misplaced.

Yet despite some unfair kinks in federal contracting procedures, the truth is that the playing field isn't all that slanted against faith-based groups. Organizations like Catholic Charities and Lutheran Social Services have been mainstay providers of social services and have received government funding for decades. Instead of acknowledging this fact, the administration indulges in rhetoric that is almost a parody of left-wing identity politics—including making false accusations of discrimination. For example, the Department of Housing and Urban Development's audit of its dealings with religious groups reports that no faith-based organizations received funding under the department's $20 million Self-Help Homeownership Opportunity Program. HUD apparently forgot that Habitat for Humanity—which has received over half of that program's total funding in recent years—is a faith-based organization. The same report concludes that religious organizations were "banned" from being owners of housing projects under a Section 202 housing program for the elderly. Again, religious groups have comprised more than two-thirds of the program's sponsoring organizations during the program's 35-year history.

Far from offsetting any serious anti-religious discrimination, the new faith-based grant program seems to have devolved into a religious version of race-based set-aside programs. As *The American Prospect* first reported [in 2003], some states that are responsible for dispersing federal social service grants have altered their grant applications to include a box that potential grantees should check to indicate whether they are faith-based. In Massachusetts, several long-time recipients of funds for programs to help veterans learned the hard way that failure to check that box leads to the sudden denial of cash. When they identified themselves as "faith-based" the next time around, their applications were, not surprisingly, approved.

Some Bush officials are alarmingly honest about this quota-like system. When I asked Courtney McCormick, deputy director of the Department of Agriculture's faith-based office, what steps the administration is taking to track the effectiveness of faith-based grantees, she candidly replied, "That's not our concern." What they do care about, she said, is "getting more churches and community groups through the door to get access to funding.". . .

A Different Kind of Republican

On the third night of the [2004] Republican convention, one of the many gauzy "W" video-mercials that appeared on giant screens in the middle of Madison Square Garden during slow stretches featured images of Bush surrounded by people of color, while in a voiceover the president reminded viewers, "I rallied the armies of compassion." More than with any other piece of his domestic policy agenda, Bush has linked himself personally to the faith-based initiative. During a campaign stop in March [2004], he told a crowd of religious leaders that he—and he alone—was responsible for the changes that have taken place. "Congress wouldn't act," Bush said, "so I signed an executive order—that means I did it on my own."

And so he did. Bush alone is responsible for supporting the distribution of taxpayer dollars without requiring proof that the funding produces results, for establishing a new government bureaucracy to give special help to a "discriminated" community that has always been on equal footing with everyone else, and for encouraging religious organizations to rely on government funding instead of encouraging private donations. It turns out that a "compassionate conservative" is a different kind of Republican after all. Just not the kind we expected.

Periodical Bibliography

The following articles have been selected to supplement the diverse views presented in this chapter.

Arthur C. Brooks	"Religious Faith and Charitable Giving," *Policy Review*, October/November 2003.
Joseph A. Califano Jr.	"Caught Between God and Caesar," *America*, June 21, 2004.
Economist	"The Triumph of the Religious Right—American Values," November 13, 2004.
Jean Bethke Elshtain	"Against Liberal Monism," *Daedalus*, Summer 2003.
Susan Jacoby	"In Praise of Secularism," *Nation*, April 19, 2004.
Wendy Kaminer	"The Real Danger Behind the Christian Right," *Free Inquiry*, October/November 2003.
Gerald F. Kreyche	"Fundamentalism and All That Jazz," *USA Today Magazine*, January 2004.
David Masci	"Religion and Politics," *CQ Researcher*, July 30, 2004.
Kenneth Minogue	"Fundamentalism Isn't the Problem," *New Criterion*, June 2004.
Chris Mooney	"W.'s Christian Nation: How Bush Promotes Religion and Erodes the Separation of Church and State," *American Prospect*, June 2003.
Anthony M. Pilla	"The Church and Democracy: The Importance of Religious Values and Institutions for Our Community and Society," *Vital Speeches of the Day*, March 15, 2002.
John M. Powers	"Mainline Churches Face Great Divide," *Insight on the News*, December 22, 2003.
Mariah Richardson-Osgood	"Bush's Faith-Based Legacy," *Humanist*, September/October 2004.
Louise Witt	"Whose Side Is God On?" *American Demographics*, February 1, 2004.

CHAPTER 3

What Should Be Done to Accommodate Religious Freedom in America?

Chapter Preface

For more than one hundred years, millions of students and teachers in public schools across the United States have started the school day by reciting the Pledge of Allegiance. Since its creation in 1892, the Pledge has undergone several revisions, with the most notable change occurring in 1954, when Congress added the words "under God" as a modifier of "one nation." This change was enacted at the height of the Cold War, when the United States wanted to emphasize its opposition to the "godless" Soviet Union. While "under God" was not very controversial in the 1950s, half a century later it ended up at the center of a heated debate between the U.S. government and a man named Michael Newdow.

In the late 1990s Newdow, an emergency-room physician with a law degree, was disturbed to discover that his five-year-old daughter was reciting the teacher-led Pledge every morning at her elementary school. While his daughter had not objected to participating in the Pledge exercise, Newdow contended that its inclusion of "under God" was an unconstitutional endorsement of religion that contradicted his atheist worldview. "For those who do not share the majority's religious belief that there exists a God—and who wish to instill nonmonotheistic values in their children—[the Pledge] intrudes into their rights of parenthood," Newdow argued. Representing himself, he took his case to a local district court, which ruled against him. His appeal to the Ninth Circuit U.S. Court of Appeals, however, was successful. In 2002 this higher court struck down the policy of the Elk Grove Unified School District, which had endorsed voluntary Pledge recitation as part of its patriotic observance policy. In turn the school district appealed the ruling to the U.S. Supreme Court.

The school district noted that Newdow's daughter was a willing reciter of the Pledge. Even if she had opposed the Pledge, the district argued, her exposure to other students' willing recitation of the Pledge could not be construed as a violation of the First Amendment's Establishment Clause (which prohibits governmental endorsement of religion). According to Terence J. Cassidy, counsel of record for the school district, "The Pledge . . . does not result in students being subjected to a religious act or statement of religious belief. The Pledge is simply a patriotic expression that includes a reference to God, which reflects a long-standing philosophy of government. Ceremonial references to God . . . have repeatedly been recognized by [the Supreme] Court to be consistent with the Establishment Clause."

In June 2004 the Supreme Court dismissed the case, arguing that Newdow could not act as his daughter's legal representative because he did not have sole custody of her. Since the girl's mother had not objected to the inclusion of "under God" in the Pledge, the decision of the Ninth Circuit Court of Appeals was reversed. However, since the Supreme Court's decision was based on a technicality, the question of the constitutionality of the Pledge remains unresolved. A future case will probably reignite this debate.

Michael Newdow's campaign is just one example of the controversy that can occur among a religiously diverse population guided by secular laws. The authors in the following chapter continue this discussion about the constitutionality of the Pledge and how to best accommodate religious freedom in schools and in the workplace.

"Freedoms . . . are undermined when a religious concept not shared by all Americans is injected into our great patriotic oath."

"Under God" Should Be Removed from the Pledge of Allegiance

Part I: Americans United for Separation of Church and State et al.; Part II: Nebraska Zen Center et al.

Requiring students to recite the Pledge of Allegiance is unconstitutional because it includes the phrase "under God," the authors of the following two-part viewpoint contend. In Part I Americans United for Separation of Church and State and the American Civil Liberties Union maintain that the Pledge pressures schoolchildren to profess religious belief, which violates the Constitution's clause against government endorsement of religion. In Part II a group representing over 3 million Buddhist Americans argues that the Pledge is incompatible with Buddhism because it expresses a belief in monotheism. Both parts of this viewpoint were submitted to the U.S. Supreme Court as amici curiae ("friends of the court") briefs in the case of *Newdow v. U.S. Congress et al.*

As you read, consider the following questions:

1. According to Americans United for Separation of Church and State, what year was "under God" added to the Pledge of Allegiance?
2. How many Buddhists are there in the United States, according to the authors of Part II?

Part I: Americans United for a Separation of Church and State et al., Amicus Curiae Brief, *Newdow v. U.S. Congress et al.*, U.S. Supreme Court, Washington, DC, February 13, 2004. Part II: Nebraska Zen Center et al., Amicus Curiae Brief, *Newdow v. U.S. Congress et al.*, U.S. Supreme Court, Washington, DC, February 12, 2004.

I

In 1943, in the darkest hours of World War II, the Court took the wrenching step of striking down a school board policy compelling schoolchildren to salute the flag, a step the Court had decisively rejected only three years earlier. The Court took this step because it concluded that the First Amendment forbids the government to compel individuals to proclaim allegiance to the political beliefs expressed in the Pledge.

The school district policy now under review [in 2004] is also constitutionally flawed, though in a different way than the policy invalidated in 1943. Since 1954, the Pledge has expressed allegiance to religious as well as political beliefs. Although the First Amendment allows the government to promote patriotism as long as participation is not compelled, the Establishment Clause forbids the government to endorse religion or pressure schoolchildren, even indirectly, to proclaim religious belief. The policy under review does both and is therefore unconstitutional.

A Ceremony of Assent

Unlike other historical and cultural texts, the Pledge is an expression of personal belief and commitment. Its recitation, as the Court has recognized, is a "ceremony of assent."— *West Virginia State Board of Education v. Barnette* (1943). The qualities ascribed to the Republic for which the flag stands are not descriptive but aspirational, and to recite the Pledge is to subscribe to those aspirations. *Barnette* rejected the contention that the qualities the Pledge ascribes to the Republic are simply "acknowledgments" of historical fact.

Since 1954, the "ceremony of assent" has included an expression of belief in "God" and devotion to a nation "under God." This is how schoolchildren would naturally understand the Pledge, how social science research indicates schoolchildren actually understand the Pledge, and how Congress meant schoolchildren to understand the Pledge. In adding "under God" to the Pledge, Congress intended to make its recitation an affirmation of religious belief. The 1954 law adding "under God" to the Pledge made affirmation of religious belief an official element of patriotism and

120

religiosity an official element of national identity. Reciting the Pledge thus became a religious exercise—not because it refers to "God," but because it is a pledge.

EGUSD's [Elk Grove Unified School District's] Pledge policy violates the Establishment Clause both because it communicates to schoolchildren a forbidden message of government endorsement of religion and because, like the school-prayer policies invalidated by the Court beginning with *Engel v. Vitale* (1962), EGUSD's policy pressures schoolchildren to profess religious belief and affirm religious ideals. Indeed, the policy pressures schoolchildren to profess a particular religious doctrine, monotheism, thereby violating the Clause's command of neutrality among religions. And by yoking patriotism to religion, EGUSD's policy exerts an even greater coercive pressure than the school-prayer policies, forcing schoolchildren to choose between declaring religious belief and being branded religious and political outsiders.

II

When children from Buddhist homes across the United States recite the Pledge of Allegiance, they utter a phrase that is inconsistent and incompatible with the religious beliefs and ethical principles they are taught by their parents, by other adults in their communities, and by their teachers at after-school religious programs and at Sunday Dharma school. That phrase is that this is a nation "under God."

Although these children may wish to say the Pledge, express their patriotism, and state aloud their commitment to this "indivisible" country and the values of "liberty and justice for all" represented by the flag, they can only do so by referring to a deity and a particular religious paradigm that is at odds with their Buddhist beliefs.

Violating the Establishment Clause

Unlike the religious group considered by the Court in *West Virginia State Board of Education v. Barnette* (1943), Buddhism does not prohibit Buddhists from committing their allegiance to the United States (indeed, numerous Buddhist Americans have given their lives fighting for this country). Thus, when viewed from a Buddhist perspective, there is no question that teacher-led recitation of the Pledge in public schools violates the very "touchstone of Establishment Clause jurisprudence: Neither a State, nor the Federal Government can pass laws which aid one religion, aid all religions, or prefer one religion over another."—*Lee v. Weisman* (1992).

Constitutional Transgressions

When Congress placed "in God We Trust" on all our coins and currency, when it inserted "under God" into the Pledge of Allegiance, when the Supreme Court starts its sessions with "God save the United States and this honorable court," when presidents take their oaths of office with chaplains offering prayers to God, when every legislative session begins with a prayer to God—and on and on—those who disbelieve in a supreme being are explicitly told that "they are outsiders, not full members of the political community," while theistic Americans are told "that they are insiders, favored members of the political community." That language—repeated time and again by the Supreme Court in describing Establishment Clause violations—details exactly what has been occurring with increasing frequency in our society.

Michael Newdow, *Free Inquiry*, Winter 2002–2003.

The United States and the *amici* senators and congressmen fail to mention Buddhism and this country's 3,000,000 to 4,000,000 Buddhists in their briefs, although they discuss the role of other religions in shaping our country's history. Buddhism has a rich history in the United States, and Buddhism is growing quickly in this country. Yet, when public school teachers lead children in reciting the Pledge, the unmistakable message conveyed by the government is that Buddhism is an outcast religion and that Buddhist students "are outsiders, not full members of the political community, and [there is] an accompanying message to adherents that they are insiders, favored members of the political community."—*Santa Fe Independent School District v. Doe* (2000).

It is irrelevant that recitation of the Pledge in public elementary and secondary schools is voluntary, because the nature of the exercise itself creates a constitutionally unacceptable dilemma for Buddhist schoolchildren. Reciting the Pledge is incompatible with Buddhist beliefs because it affirms loyalty to a nation "under God." However, if Buddhist schoolchildren adhere to their religious beliefs and remain silent, they are denied the opportunity for patriotic expression by reciting the Pledge. They also run the risk of being stigmatized and branded as unpatriotic.

Whether or not they participate in the Pledge, Buddhist schoolchildren are confronted with a vision of their country that is "under God," and therefore irreconcilable with their religion. The dilemma for Buddhist schoolchildren created by the Pledge constitutes coercion and the endorsement by the government of a particular religion in violation of the Establishment Clause under the Court's precedents, particularly *Lee* and *Santa Fe.*

Undermining Freedoms

The Pledge cannot be justified as mere "ceremonial deism," nor can it be characterized as a history lesson, nor can it be dismissed as a *de minimis* affront to Buddhists that they must tolerate because other Americans hold monotheistic beliefs. The 1954 amendment to the Pledge, however well-intentioned, was a mistake that unconstitutionally entwined the government with Judeo-Christian monotheism and breached the "wall of separation between church and state."—*Reynolds v. United States* (1978).

The very freedoms that the American flag represents, and the very sense of national unity that teacher-led recitation of the Pledge is intended to foster, are undermined when a religious concept not shared by all Americans is injected into our great patriotic oath.

"The attack on the Pledge of Allegiance is but another way station on the road to a post-Christian America."

"Under God" Should Remain in the Pledge of Allegiance

Steve Bonta

In the following viewpoint Steve Bonta denounces the attempt to remove the phrase "under God" from the Pledge of Allegiance. Since God is the source of all individual rights, governments that publicly acknowledge the supremacy of God are the truest defenders of liberty, claims Bonta. Governments that do not exalt God, however, squelch individual virtue and enable the triumph of amorality and tyranny. While it is true that the Constitution forbids governmental establishment of religion, this prohibition was intended to prevent a particular sect from becoming the national religion, not to banish all religion from the state, Bonta contends. Bonta is a writer for the *New American*, a biweekly conservative journal.

As you read, consider the following questions:
1. Who is Michael Newdow, according to the author?
2. What specific example does Bonta use to illustrate what happens to governments that refuse to acknowledge the supremacy of God?
3. What U.S. Supreme Court decisions have "exiled" Christian culture from public life, in Bonta's opinion?

The late, great comedian Red Skelton once remarked on national TV, concerning the Pledge of Allegiance, "Since I was a small boy . . . two words have been added to the Pledge . . . : 'under God.' Wouldn't it be a pity if someone said 'That is a prayer,' and [the Pledge] would be eliminated from schools too?" Mr. Skelton, an entertainer speaking to another age, when patriotism and public expressions of faith were still very much in fashion, would be dismayed to see his prediction close to becoming reality. On June 26th [2002], the Ninth Circuit Court of Appeals ruled in favor of plaintiff Michael Newdow, a militant atheist who had sued the federal government to require that the Pledge of Allegiance be prohibited in public schools because it refers to God.[1]

Yet even in 1969, when Red Skelton voiced his concern, the drive, spearheaded by the federal judiciary, to banish religion completely from public life was already far advanced. And just as Skelton could foresee where the trend to secularize public schools might lead, so we can easily imagine future frontiers for the dogmatic enemies of religion to explore. Is it a stretch to imagine future monetary currency purged of all references to God, as Michael Newdow also advocates (he makes a practice of crossing out "In God We Trust" on all paper currency that passes through his hands)? How about a future Congress shorn of chaplains and prayers? Or even future courts of law in which the phrase "so help me God" has been removed from the oath required of witnesses? In an age where Christmas displays and the Ten Commandments have been banned from public buildings and public prayer from school sporting events, the attack on the Pledge of Allegiance is but another way station on the road to a post-Christian America.

It wasn't always thus. During the founding era, Americans almost unanimously ascribed their success, first in winning independence from the British, and then in creating a constitutional republic, to divine intervention. The founding generation regarded God both as involved in the affairs of the American republic and as the supreme Source of authority to whom all governments must defer.

1. In 2004 the case went to the U.S. Supreme Court, which dismissed Newdow's challenge because of a legal technicality.

God Is the Source of Rights

If ever there were a first principle of political thought, a bedrock premise on which all other political, legal, and social reasoning should be founded, it is that God is the Source of all rights. As with the physical creation, so with the spiritual and the moral: God is the final cause and origin of all things pertaining to man. As the Declaration of Independence states so emphatically, He endows men with "certain unalienable Rights," among which are "Life, Liberty, and the Pursuit of Happiness.". . .

Republican governments under God . . . are the truest champions of liberty. God, the source of all of man's attributes, obviously has created us with varied and unequal endowments of talents. Under conditions of liberty, men and women of equal God-given rights deploy their diverse and unequal God-given skills to create a society where every individual benefits from the talents of others.

Government Without God

When God is removed from the calculus of government, all of these attributes of God-given liberty are turned on their heads. It was the French Revolution, that grotesque parody of the American founding, which first enshrined the heresy that rights are transmitted to the individual, not by God, but by the Almighty Collective or "general will." According to the French Declaration of the Rights of Man and Citizen, the counterfeit of our glorious Declaration of Independence, all sovereignty (i.e., power) resides "essentially in the nation. No group, no individual may exercise authority not emanating expressly therefrom." The French sansculottes, in substituting for God the will of the majority, completely inverted the relationship of individual to state. Government, which they believed to have originated by majoritarian consent, conferred rights on individuals, reserving to itself the power to revise or retract them any time it chose.

From this distorted premise flow distorted ideas, which have been responsible for much of man's suffering at the hands of the State. For if there is no God, then the State must reign supreme, and all must obey its edicts. Morality then becomes mere obedience to man-made, positive law, and subject to change at the whims of rulers. Instead of equality under the law, egalitarianism—the radical urge to suppress and level individual achievement—becomes the order of the day. Among the clamoring interest groups that replace individuals as the fundamental political units, strength depends on conformity to mass standards rather than on independent thought and action. Moreover, since individuals are no longer the crucial building blocks on which government depends, personal virtue and self-discipline are no longer needed. Such government does not have liberty as its goal, but seeks instead to exercise raw force. It must therefore be freed from all moral, legal, and religious restraints to achieve its full destructive potential.

Wright. © 2003 by Tribune Media Services. Reproduced by permission.

These two great polarities are completely irreconcilable. Either men will serve God, and frame government to protect God-given rights, thereby maximizing human liberty, or they will serve the exalted State, the most powerful agency man can create when left to his own devices. Only a State acknowledging God as an authority superior to itself will resist the tidal pull of tyranny.

Church and State

But then what of the Founders' insistence, in the First Amendment to the U.S. Constitution, on Congress making "no law respecting an establishment of religion, or prohibiting the free exercise thereof"? Doesn't this mean that a "wall of separation between church and state," in Jefferson's famous phrase, should be erected at every level of government?

First, there is an important distinction between a "church" or an "established religion," on one hand, and "religion" in general on the other. The phrase "established religion" referred in the Founders' day to an official or state religion such as the Church of England. Both the Founders and the English jurist William Blackstone, whose writings on English law were widely read by the Founders, often used such terminology. Blackstone, in his *Commentaries on the Laws of England*, wrote of England's established church:

> If . . . men quarrel with the ecclesiastical establishment, the civil magistrate has nothing to do with it. . . . [But the civil magistrate] is bound to protect the established church. . . . For, if every sect were to be indulged in a free communion of civil employments, the idea of a national establishment would at once be destroyed, and the Episcopal church would no longer be the church of England.

The First Amendment, then, prohibits not the public exercise of faith but the establishment by law of a particular sect as the official national religion. The Founders had no intention of banishing Christianity in general from the halls of government; they saw their country and the government they had founded as essentially Christian. . . .

Secularizing the State

Unfortunately, with the advance of militant secularism in the 20th century, the government in general and the Supreme Court in particular began looking for ways to exclude religion from the public domain altogether. . . .

In 1962, the Supreme Court, in *Engel v. Vitale*, inexplicably discovered a constitutional prohibition on prayer in public schools. From that day to this, America has been barraged with court decisions similar in tone to *Engel*, effectively exiling Christian culture, morality, and symbolism from public life. We've seen court decrees banning prayer at school athletic events, mandating the removal of creches and Christmas decorations from government property, and ordering displays of the Ten Commandments in courtrooms to be taken down. At the same time, the courts have protected the alleged rights of the vilest of pornographers, abortionists, and political subversives to ply their nefarious trades. In effect, the government is not driving religion per se out of government, but merely replacing Judeo-Christian values with the humanistic doctrine of exalted, amoral Man. . . .

Michael Newdow, with his incoherent claims of constitutional support for his crusade against the Pledge of Allegiance, is only the latest anti-religious extremist granted a hearing by the modern American secularist establishment. His ludicrous claims—that "it's my parental right to keep the government off my child" (even as he insists on allowing the government to educate his child in public school), and that "the Constitution says that the government isn't supposed to be infusing religion into our society"—don't deserve to be dignified by further comment here.

But unfortunately, many Americans now believe, at least in part, the outrageous fallacies and distortions about religion and government foisted on them by the media and public schools, and dutifully retailed by the likes of Newdow. We are, tragically, well on our way to becoming a post-Christian civilization.

America, however, cannot deny God's supremacy and remain free. To drift away from our Christian moorings is to chart a course into bondage, both spiritual and political. The French Revolutionaries and others of their ilk began by erecting secular, even anti-Christian states glorifying Man, and ended up enslaving themselves under mob rule, guided and harnessed by tyrants and demagogues. For us there can be no middle ground; we either mimic the mistakes of those who turned their backs on their Creator, or keep both ourselves and our government subservient to the supreme Law-giver, remaining, as our Founders hoped, one nation under God.

"An understanding of the role of religion in history, art, and current events is necessary for a well-rounded education."

Public Schools Should Encourage Instruction About Religion

Krista Kafer

Public school students have the right to receive instruction about religion and its role in history, writes Krista Kafer in the following viewpoint. When teachers use instructional methods that are academic rather than devotional, the study of religion enhances cross-cultural sensitivity and promotes a deeper understanding of other disciplines, Kafer maintains. Students also have the right to express religious beliefs, to form religious clubs, and to pray, as long as these activities are student led and do not infringe on the rights of others. Public schools that want to ensure a well-rounded education for their students should provide them with opportunities to learn about religion, she concludes. Kafer is an education policy analyst at the Heritage Foundation, a public policy research institute.

As you read, consider the following questions:
1. How did the Modesto, California, school district prepare their teachers for instruction about religion, according to Kafer?
2. According to the author, why did the Excelsior School draw criticism for its course on Islam?
3. What is the Equal Access Act of 1984, according to Kafer?

Krista Kafer, "How to Teach Religion in Public Schools," *The World & I Online*, vol. 17, August 2002. Copyright © 2002 by News World Communications, Inc. Reproduced by permission.

E arlier this year [2002], a kindergartner named Kayla was told she couldn't pray with her friends during lunch. Her family filed suit against her New York school district, and a federal judge ordered the school to allow the girl to pray while the trial proceeds.

This situation probably never would have arisen if school officials had been properly cognizant of a string of Supreme Court decisions in recent decades that have clarified students' rights and responsibilities under the law regarding religious exercise and free speech. Ignorance of these decisions has led to school policies, as in Kayla's case, that chill legal religious practice and that cold-shoulder the legitimate and legal teaching *about* religion in such subjects as social studies, literature, history, and geography.

According to the Constitution, the American people are guaranteed the right to practice religion free from government intervention. But interpreting the First Amendment clause "Congress shall make no law respecting an establishment of religion, or prohibiting the free exercise thereof" has not been easy, particularly pertaining to public schools. Nonetheless, the High Court has said, generally speaking, that voluntary student expression and the study of religion are protected but proselytizing and school-sanctioned or teacher-led prayers are not.

Students' First Amendment Rights

The justices have recognized students' First Amendment rights to religious expression and to receive instruction about religion and its role in history, philosophy, and the arts. Congress has voted to enforce—and the Court has affirmed—the right of student religious groups to receive the same access and treatment as other groups. These distinctions are well articulated in a 1995 statement of principles by the National Education Association (NEA), the country's largest teachers union, the Christian Coalition, and 22 other educational associations and religious groups.

"Public schools may not inculcate nor inhibit religion," the document says. "They must be places where religion and religious conviction are treated with fairness and respect. Public schools uphold the First Amendment when they protect the religious liberty rights of students of all faiths or none. Schools demonstrate fairness when they ensure that the curriculum includes study about religion, where appropriate, as an important part of a complete education."

While student religious expression and academic instruction about religion are constitutional, school policies vary in the degree to which they are allowed in practice. Some schools provide an open, balanced environment in which students can learn about religions and express their religious beliefs. Other school policies have not been consistent with the law.

Thus, it is essential for educators, administrators, parents, and students to understand their rights and responsibilities under the law and to work together to create a school environment that is both consistent with the Constitution and educationally beneficial for all children.

Teaching About Religion

Religion has played a significant part in history and the arts and continues to do so in the world today. Thus, a wide spectrum of experts contends that religion belongs in a well-rounded curriculum. They say it is essential to understanding the various academic disciplines and developing cross-cultural sensitivity. For example, the late Justice William Brennan, in a concurring opinion in *Abington v. Schempp*, stated that "it would be impossible to teach meaningfully many subjects in the social sciences or the humanities without some mention of religion."

Many educator groups concur. NEA Resolution E-7 says, "The National Education Association believes that educational materials should accurately portray the influence of religion in our nation and throughout the world." The National Council for the Social Studies Curriculum Standards declares: "Knowledge about religions is not only a characteristic of an educated person but is absolutely necessary for understanding and living in a world of diversity. Knowledge of religious differences and the role of religion in the contemporary world can help promote understanding and alleviate prejudice."

The Modesto, California, public school district offers a

strong example of how schools can teach about religion. When the district launched a ninth-grade comparative religions class, it ensured that the teachers were well prepared. They worked to give teachers a solid understanding of First Amendment issues and content. Teachers attended workshops that included notable scholars. The district understood the importance of the topic and ensured that it would be constitutional and enriching for students.

Many states have established standards recommending the teaching of religion in social studies, the arts, and literature. California, for example, requires teaching about religions in its History–Social Science Framework. Additionally, the California County Superintendents Educational Services Association and the First Amendment Center sponsor a statewide program called the California 3Rs Project, which conducts seminars, forums, and workshops on teaching about religions and student religious liberties. The project supports constitutional and educationally beneficial practices and promotes the "three Rs": rights, responsibilities, and respect in California's diverse school environments. Several other states have initiated 3Rs projects as well.

Religion Teaching's Constitutionality

In California, teachers may teach about the role of religion in history, its artistic influence, significant events, basic tenets, and important figures. The same court case that denied state-sponsored school prayer affirmed instruction about religion. As outlined in Associate Justice Tom Clark's opinion in *Abington v. Schempp*: "It might well be said that one's education is not complete without a study of comparative religion or the history of religion and its relationship to the advancement of civilization. It certainly may be said that the Bible is worthy of study for its literary and historic qualities. Nothing we have said here indicates that such study of the Bible or of religion, when presented objectively as part of a secular program of education, may not be effected consistently with the First Amendment."

Permissible instruction includes such subjects as the history of religion, the role of religion in U.S. or world history, comparative religion, sacred texts, including the Bible as literature, and the study of sacred music and art. The instructional approach must be academic rather than devotional. It should neither denigrate nor promote beliefs or practices. The goal should be to teach knowledge and understanding about religions without favoring any particular faith. Instruction can include a study of central beliefs, symbols, prominent figures, and events. Students should be able to discuss their beliefs in an atmosphere free of denigration. If a student asks a teacher about his or her religious beliefs, it is permissible to give a brief answer, however, such a moment should not be used to proselytize for or against religion.

Liberal Reasons for Studying Religion

There are good liberal, secular reasons for incorporating the serious study of religion into the curriculum of public schools. . . . A good liberal education should expose students to the major ways that humankind has devised for thinking about what is most important. Some of those ways are religious. Religions continue to possess a great deal of intellectual vitality, even in our secular culture. They continue to ask and provide answers to those existential questions on which any educated person must reflect. Theologians—conservative and liberal—continue to provide alternatives to secular ways of thinking about the world. . . .

How to incorporate the serious study of religion into the curriculum is, of course, controversial and complex. But religious voices (conservative and liberal, Christian and non-Christian) must be included in the curricular conversation, not to save religion, but to be consistent with our educational, political, and constitutional principles.

Warren A. Nord, *Christian Century*, July 14, 1999.

Teachers may expose students to primary sources. When guest speakers are invited to speak in the classroom, the content of their speeches should be academic rather than promotional. Educators should use care in choosing learning activities. The California 3Rs Project cautions educators not to use methods, such as role-playing, that could risk "blurring the legal distinction between constitutional teaching *about* religion and school-sponsored practice of religion, which is prohibited by the First Amendment to the U.S. Constitution."

In January [2002], Excelsior School in the Byron Union

School District near Oakland, California, drew criticism for its three-week course on Islam. Seventh-graders adopted Muslim names, read verses from the Qur'an, learned to write Islamic proverbs in Arabic, and organized a pretend hajj, or journey to Mecca. The course handout read, "From the beginning, you and your classmates will become Muslims." In response, the California 3Rs Project cautioned educators that

> role-playing religious practices runs the risk of trivializing and caricaturing the religion that is being studied. It's more respectful and educationally sound to view a video of real Muslims practicing their faith than having a group of seventh-graders pretend to be Muslims. . . . Role-playing runs the risk of putting students in the position of participating in activities that may violate their (or their parents') consciences. Such an issue doesn't arise when teachers teach about religion by assigning research, viewing videos, and through class instruction rather than organizing activities that may be easily perceived, rightly or wrongly, as promoting students' participation in a religious practice.

Although the law does not permit the celebration of religious holidays in school, it does permit teaching about religious holidays. Instruction may include the use of religious symbols, sacred music, literature, art, and drama. Such activities must have academic or aesthetic value and be used to promote knowledge and understanding rather than religious conviction. It is appropriate, for example, to hold a concert that includes a variety of secular and sacred music from diverse traditions. Student-created artwork with religious symbols is permissible, but teachers should not encourage or discourage the content of the artwork.

Off-Campus Religious Classes

Religious instruction may occur during school hours off campus. Twenty-nine states currently have "released-time" programs that allow students to attend weekly classes on religion. Designed by the local community, programs may include the study and memorization of sacred texts, or discussion of topics like character, peer pressure, or substance abuse. Typically, programs provide an hour a week of instruction for students in grades K–6. Some states have daily high school–level programs.

The Supreme Court's 1952 *Zorach v. Clauson* decision affirmed the constitutionality of released-time religious education. Programs must be voluntary and off-site, and students must have parental permission. Sponsors provide transportation and assume liability for participating students.

Student Religious Expression

Religious speech is protected under the Constitution. Students may express religious beliefs in the classroom and during noninstructional hours, so long as they do not infringe on the rights of other students or disrupt school proceedings. Expression includes speech, artwork, written assignments, and even clothing. Students are permitted to pray individually and in groups. They may read sacred texts and discuss religion with other willing students. Students are allowed to wear clothing with religious messages if apparel with secular messages or symbols meets the dress code. They may distribute religious literature under the same terms that govern the distribution of non-school-related literature.

In general, religious student groups have the same liberties as secular student groups. The Equal Access Act of 1984 protects student-led religious groups in public secondary schools that receive federal funds and allow nonacademic groups to meet on school grounds. Under the law, religious student groups must be accorded the same access, resources, or recognition as other student organizations. If a school-spirit club or a chess team meets after school in a classroom, the school must give faith-based clubs the same right to meet. The only difference is that religious groups must be initiated and led solely by students. Teachers may monitor them but may not participate. Teachers may participate in religious activities, such as prayer, alone or with other teachers outside of the presence of students.

[In 2001], the Supreme Court extended the right of access to private community organizations in *Good News Club v. Milford Central School*. If other community groups such as the Girl Scouts or 4-H Clubs are permitted on campus, religious activity groups must also be allowed to meet. The decision says that speech with an explicit religious message is as constitutionally protected as other speech.

Religious expression is not only constitutional; according to many experts, it is also beneficial. Creating a space for religious expression, they say, can improve the school environment. They say that such policies recognize the value of religious expression, show respect for students' deeply held beliefs, and build trust between parents and schools.

[In November 2001], during the Muslim holy month of Ramadan, New York City Schools Chancellor Harold Levy issued a statement affirming students' rights to religious expression of all faiths and urging schools to show sensitivity to requests for religious accommodation. He stated, "Tolerance for religious devotion is one of the hallmarks of our democracy. I would ask that during these difficult times all staff continue to be vigilant in both respecting religious beliefs and protecting fundamental constitutional principles." Levy's respect for students' religious beliefs and expression provided an example for other educators following the tragic events of September 11, 2001.

Schools need not be and, legally speaking, should not be "religion-free" zones. The Supreme Court has affirmed students' rights to religious expression and the appropriateness of instruction about religion. An understanding of the role of religion in history, art, and current events is necessary for a well-rounded education. Religious expression is protected for students of every faith. They are free to pray and otherwise practice their religion so long as it is not disruptive. Released time provides students with the opportunity for religious instruction off campus. Religious groups by law must be accorded the same treatment as secular groups on campus.

Knowing the law is the first step toward building equitable end constitutional school policies. Resources are available to help educators, parents, students, and communities. The Department of Education, the Freedom Forum First Amendment Center, the Family Research Council, and the NEA, for example, have information on their Web sites.

Opening of dialogue between schools, parents, and community groups can help promote understanding and support for these school policies and programs. In a 1999 letter to educators, then–Secretary of Education Richard Riley advised that "in developing such a policy, school officials can engage parents, teachers, the various faith communities, and the broader community in a positive dialogue to define a common ground that gives all parties the assurance that when questions do arise regarding religious expression the community is well prepared to apply these guidelines to specific cases."

Supported by the law and the community, schools can create numerous opportunities for learning and expression in public schools. Through these opportunities, students will gain a more well-rounded education and a greater appreciation for the diverse religious heritage of other students.

"*In recent years, Religious Right groups have been pushing the envelope and trying to introduce sectarian themes in public schools under the guise of teaching about religion.*"

Public Schools Must Avoid the Promotion of Religion

Rob Boston

Public schools need to be on the lookout for Religious Right activists who try to proselytize in public schools while claiming to be teaching objectively about religion, argues Rob Boston in the following viewpoint. Some Religious Right groups even invite teachers to adopt sectarian approaches in their classrooms without receiving administrative approval, he points out. Such teacher-initiated indoctrination of students is unconstitutional and unfair to believers and nonbelievers alike. Boston is an activist for Americans United for Separation of Church and State and the author of several books, including *Close Encounters with the Religious Right.*

As you read, consider the following questions:

1. What was sophomore Ashley Heckman's first reading assignment in her world history class, according to the author?
2. What is the significance of the landmark Supreme Court case *Abington Township School District v. Schempp,* according to Boston?
3. According to Boston, what have been some of Focus on the Family's recommendations to public school teachers?

Rob Boston, "When Teachers Preach: Student's Lawsuit Challenged Missouri School District's Religious Bias," *Church & State*, vol. 56, June 2003, pp. 7–8. Copyright © 2003 by Americans United for Separation of Church and State. Reproduced by permission.

It didn't take long for Evelyn Welk to suspect that something was amiss in her 16-year-old daughter's World History class.

Two days into the class, Welk's daughter, Ashley Heckman, a sophomore at Truman High School in Independence, Mo., came home with her first reading assignment: A two-page excerpt from a sermon by the late fundamentalist Southern Baptist preacher W.A. Criswell titled "The Hoaxes of Anthropology."

The sermon, first delivered by Criswell in 1957, ridicules the findings of modern anthropology and attacks evolution.

"This sermon debunked anthropological information," Welk said. "I saw it as someone trying to impose a religious ideology. An attack on evolution should not be part of a history class."

Welk was further alarmed later in the year when Ashley told her the class had watched a video about the birth and early life of Jesus Christ. The video, "Jesus and His Times: The Story Begins," was produced by the Reader's Digest Association in 1991. While the video does not take a strictly devotional approach, Welk was upset because it tends to present Jesus' birth and early life, as recorded in the Books of Luke and Matthew, as factual.

Slanted Toward Christianity

Welk contends that other aspects of teacher Chris Earley's classroom instruction were slanted toward Christianity. The doctrines of other religions, when taught, were prefaced with statements like "Muslims believe" and "Buddhists believe," she said, while "Christian doctrines were stated as fact."

As an example, Welk notes that the Paganism of the early Greeks and the rise of Judaism were barely discussed in the class. By contrast, when the class talked about the Roman Empire, Welk said, Earley spent most of the time discussing the life of Jesus and the Christianization of Rome, even though for the vast majority of its history the Roman Empire was officially Pagan.

Welk met with Earley, Principal Michael Jeffers and other school officials to resolve the problem but believed she was making little headway. The school officials, she [said], were convinced that their activities were in line with the law.

"They did not believe they were doing anything unconstitutional, and we did," Welk said.

During one meeting, Welk said, Earley told her he and Jeffers would eventually "convince me why they were right."

Added Welk, "During the meeting, there were numerous implications that the only moral children were Christian children. Earley said we could not teach history without teaching religion. He seemed unable to separate his religious views from the instruction. At that point, I contacted the ACLU [American Civil Liberties Union]."

Public Schools as "Mission Fields"?

There are conservative evangelists, such as Jerry Johnston and the Rev. Jerry Falwell, who have described public schools as "mission fields." In communities from coast to coast, proselytizers from well-financed national organizations, such as Campus Crusade and Young Life, and volunteer "youth pastors" from local congregations, have operated in public schools for years. They use a variety of techniques: presenting assembly programs featuring "role model" athletes, getting permission from school officials to contact students one-on-one in cafeterias and hallways, volunteering as unpaid teaching aides, and using substance abuse lectures or assemblies to gain access to students. It is not uncommon for these activities to have the tacit approval of local school authorities.

Edd Doerr, *Phi Delta Kappan*, November 1998.

ACLU officials also met with the same school officials but were unable to resolve the matter. Suspecting that the problem might end up in court, staffers at the ACLU of Kansas and Western Missouri contacted Americans United [for Separation of Church and State] and asked for help with the case.

On May 1 [2003], the two groups decided they had waited long enough and filed a lawsuit in federal court, asserting that the Independence School District had violated the First Amendment by failing to curb Earley's promotion of religion.

The *Welk v. Independence School District* case asserts that Earley used the World History course to promote his version of Christianity in several ways. It asks that the practices be terminated and that the school take steps to keep religious indoctrination out of the classroom.

Education, Not Indoctrination

Officials at Americans United [AU] point out that the organization does not oppose objective instruction about religion in public schools. Americans United has stated repeatedly that public schools can teach about religion's role in world and U.S. history without violating church-state separation. Such instruction, however, must be balanced and objective and intended to educate, not indoctrinate. Truman High, AU asserts, has stepped over the line.

"It's the job of parents, not public schools, to teach children religion," said Americans United Executive Director Barry W. Lynn. "The Constitution forbids public schools to promote Christianity or any other faith. Teachers may not abuse the public trust by pushing their personal religious agenda in the classroom."

School officials have so far refused to comment on the case. But attorneys with Americans United and the ACLU say the lawsuit is legally sound and should be resolved quickly if the judge follows existing precedent.

Numerous courts have ruled that public schools may not endorse or promote Christianity or other religions. Since the Supreme Court's rulings banning mandatory school prayer in 1962 and '63, dozens of federal courts have upheld the idea that public schools may not get into the business of teaching religion.

Furthermore, teachers do not have a free speech right to proselytize students or to urge them to adopt different religious beliefs. Allowing teachers such latitude, the courts have ruled, not only violates separation of church and state but also infringes on parental rights.

At the same time, courts have upheld the right of public schools to teach about religion in an objective manner. In the landmark 1963 school prayer case *Abington Township School District v. Schempp*, Justice Tom Clark pointed out, "[I]t might well be said that one's education is not complete without a study of comparative religion or the history of religion and its relationship to the advancement of civilization.

. . . Nothing we have said here indicates that such study of the Bible or of religion, when presented objectively as part of a secular program of education, may not be effected consistently with the First Amendment."

Blurring the Line

But the line between legitimate instruction and promotion of religion can be blurred by Religious Right activists determined to bring their faith into the classroom. In recent years, Religious Right groups have begun pushing the envelope and trying to introduce sectarian themes in public schools under the guise of teaching about religion.

In Greensboro, N.C., Elizabeth Ridenhour runs the National Council on Bible Curriculum in Public Schools, a group closely aligned with TV preacher D. James Kennedy. The Council claims it merely promotes teaching about the Bible; in fact, its curriculum reflects fundamentalist dogma and is akin to Sunday School lessons.

James Dobson's Focus on the Family has also shown great interest in this strategy. In 1998, the organization's *Teachers in Focus* magazine recommended that public school teachers engage in "modifying classroom activities, changing homework assignments, passing out supplementary readings, presenting alternative viewpoints or making other changes" to challenge "the secular status quo in the subject you teach." The publication went so far as to recommend that these steps be taken without approval from the principal.

Americans United attorneys say it's difficult to know if that's what happened in Independence. But the organization remains alert to ongoing efforts to violate church-state separation in public schools and is aware of evolving Religious Right strategies.

Abiding by the First Amendment

Responding to an inquiry from the *Kansas City Star*, officials at the Independence School District declined to comment on the case directly but did issue copies of the district's policy on religion. The policy states that "espousal of any particular religious denomination or faith is strictly forbidden" but says "teachers may teach about religion with information being presented at an appropriate maturity level for students."

The district also charged that Welk failed to follow proper procedures for challenging curriculum materials, an allegation Welk and her attorneys dispute.

In an interview, . . . Welk recounted her efforts to resolve the matter through meetings with school officials and noted that as early as [the fall of 2002] she asked the ACLU to contact the school on her behalf.

ACLU attorney John M. Simpson said he talked to officials at the school in October and December of [2002] as well as April [2003] but found them unresponsive.

"It seemed they were not doing anything, so we decided it was necessary to file a lawsuit," Simpson told the *Star.*

Welk [said] she simply wants the school to abide by the First Amendment.

"I believe in the Constitution," she said. "I think this situation is pretty blatant, and that most people of the Christian faith would not want anyone else teaching their children about religion. Separation of church and state is there for a reason."

"Many Americans of faith . . . are victims of employment discrimination due to [religious] practices and beliefs."

New Laws Are Needed to Protect Religious Freedom in the Workplace

Avi Schick

In the following viewpoint Avi Schick contends that the United States needs more laws to protect Americans of faith from antireligious discrimination in the workplace. People frequently experience such discrimination when they wear religious clothing, or request time off for religious observances, he points out. The courts have not been very helpful to workers who seek to have their religious practices accommodated—even though precedent-setting laws have been passed requiring employers to accommodate other workers, such as those with disabilities. Concerned advocates should focus their efforts on enacting antidiscrimination laws at the state level, Schick concludes. Schick is deputy counsel to New York State attorney general Eliot Spitzer.

As you read, consider the following questions:

1. What happened to several fez-wearing spectators who came to observe a trial conducted by St. Louis federal judge Michael Reagan, according to the author?
2. According to Schick, what was the outcome of the Supreme Court case of *TWA v. Hardison?*
3. What kind of protections against religious discrimination do federal workers have, according to Schick?

When French President Jacques Chirac endorsed a recent proposal to prohibit French schoolchildren from wearing religious clothing in public schools, the United States was quick to criticize him. American Ambassador John V. Hartford indignantly claimed that "a fundamental principle of religious freedom . . . is that all persons should be able to practice their religion and their beliefs peacefully, without government interference." While the ambassador's statement appears unequivocal, it skirts an issue with significant implications for religious Americans: In condemning only "government interference" with religious freedom, Hartford glossed over a simmering domestic debate about employer interference with religious practices and beliefs. This is a critical issue for the many Americans of faith who are victims of employment discrimination due to such practices and beliefs.

Workplace Discrimination

If you think the problem doesn't exist here, try wearing your turban to the St. Louis courtroom of federal judge Michael Reagan. [In 2002], Reagan threatened to evict several fez-wearing spectators who came to observe a trial. When a woman protested that she was wearing a hat to show respect for her lord, the judge told her to "please leave, take it off, and come back in, or do not come back in. The choice is yours." The judge also made it clear that he was an equal-opportunity offender. When asked whether he would have been as dismissive of more traditional religious practices, Judge Reagan replied: "Jews will not wear yarmulkes. I am Catholic, and the pope would not wear a miter."

It is hard to know why Reagan got so worked up by the sight of religious headgear, but he is not alone. [In December 2003], Sikhs gathered at the New Jersey Statehouse in Trenton to demand legislation to protect against the job discrimination they experience because they wear turbans. My boss, New York Attorney General Eliot Spitzer, had to step in a few years back when a well-known chain of hair salons fired a longtime employee after he started wearing his yarmulke on the job. And it's not just religious headgear that seems to tick off employers. Both the Equal Employment Opportunity Commission and the New York Attorney General's office sued Federal Express over its policy prohibiting employees who wear dreadlocks for religious reasons from being promoted to positions that require customer contact.

Workplace discrimination is not confined to blue-collar jobs, either. A few years ago, at a Columbia Law School forum, a partner at one of the country's largest law firms candidly observed that wearing a yarmulke to an interview will diminish one's job prospects. An informal study at Fordham Law School concluded that Jewish students on the Law Review who wore yarmulkes to their job interviews were far less likely than their classmates to be called back for a second interview. And New York law firms are far more progressive—and accommodating—than most.

Undue Hardship?

There ought to be a law. And technically, there is. In 1972, Title VII of the 1964 Civil Rights Act was amended to require employers to "reasonably accommodate" the religious practices of their employees, unless that accommodation would impose an "undue hardship" on the employer. But in 1977 the Supreme Court held, in *TWA v. Hardison*, that anything more than a very minimal cost is an "undue hardship" that negates the employers' duty to accommodate workers.

Money costs are not the only possible source of undue hardship claims. Courts have found businesses' concerns about workplace morale or even "industrial peace" to be more compelling than a religious accommodation. One federal court even relied upon the claims about the negative impact on a restaurant's public image, in dismissing a claim brought by a Sikh employee who was fired after refusing to shave his beard.

And cases involving clothing or grooming are not the most difficult. Many religious discrimination cases involve the religious employee's need for time off for religious observances. In *Hardison*, the court held that it would be an "undue hardship" to require TWA to incur a $150 cost to accommodate an employee who refused to work on his Sabbath. While some courts have subsequently rejected claims advanced by large employers that relatively minimal expenses constitute undue hardship, others have upheld them.

To be sure, nobody expects the courts to direct businesses

to incur substantial expenses to accommodate a single employee. Courts, and businesses, must draw a line beyond which accommodation is truly burdensome and therefore unnecessary. But the courts have been less than generous to religious employees when deciding where to place that line.

An Interesting Comparison

This inflexibility of courts and employers is striking in that it comes just as we have expanded the obligation to assist other members of society traditionally excluded from the workplace.

The Problem of "Undue Hardship"

Although Title VII of the 1964 Civil Rights Act requires employers to "reasonably accommodate" their employees' religious beliefs, unless doing so would impose "undue hardship" on the conduct of their business, it does not define "undue hardship."

However, a landmark 1977 U.S. Supreme Court ruling defined it as anything causing more than a *"de minimis,"* or minimal, burden. In a case involving Trans World Airlines (TWA), the court ruled the airline was not obligated to give an employee the day off to observe his Sabbath—even though the accommodation would have cost the huge company only $150.

Some legal experts argue that the TWA ruling and others like it gutted the religious rights that workers once had under Title VII. Indeed, the *de minimis* standard would allow a business to refuse an employee's request for time off to pray even though the only "hardship" it would incur would be the nominal administrative costs associated with rearranging the schedule.

Brian Hansen, *CQ Researcher*, August 23, 2002.

The most prominent manifestation of this trend is the Americans with Disabilities Act [ADA], legislation requiring employers to accommodate individuals with disabilities. Under the ADA, an employer's duty to offer a "reasonable accommodation" to the disabled includes offering "job restructuring . . . modified work schedules and reassignment to a vacant position." Claims of "undue hardship" are limited to those requiring a "significant difficulty or expense" when considered in light of the resources of the employer. In short, no major airline would be permitted to rely on a $150 cost to avoid its obligations to the handicapped under the ADA.

Why then is religious accommodation accorded second-class status under the law? For one thing, courts may be concerned that a meaningful obligation to accommodate will morph into a preference for religious practice that violates the Establishment Clause.[1] Moreover, employers often value uniformity above all else, seek out "team players," and are therefore suspicious of workers who desire to be "different." Some suspect an element of disrespect to America in the stubborn insistence of those who want to preserve the traditions they have brought from foreign lands. These concerns are misplaced. By focusing on the constitutional concerns, the current law lends objective cover to employers who seek to discriminate. And the stereotyping of religious employees is "religious profiling," which, like its discredited cousin, is a self-fulfilling process that leads to a bigoted result.

Guidelines on Religious Exercise

For several years, religious groups have been advocating legislation that would incorporate the ADA's broader definition of "reasonable accommodation" and narrower interpretation of "undue hardship" into legislation protecting the rights of religious employees. However, the bill—known as the Workplace Religious Freedom Act—is opposed by business groups and has languished in Congress. In 1997, President [Bill] Clinton conveyed his dissatisfaction with the current state of the law by issuing "Guidelines on Religious Exercise and Religious Expression in the Federal Workplace."

These guidelines offer more protection to federal workers than Title VII provides to private sector employees. For example, they state that an agency should grant an exemption from work rules that burden an employee's religious practice "unless the agency has a compelling interest in denying the exemption, and there is no less restrictive means of furthering that interest." There is also a presumption in favor of permitting employees to wear religious garb, allowing them to be banned only if they "unduly interfere with the functioning of

---

1. This is the First Amendment assertion that "Congress shall make no law respecting an establishment of religion, or prohibiting the free exercise thereof."

the workplace." Although these guidelines are binding only on federal agencies, they send a message about the inadequacy of current federal law. The states have begun to pick up on that message by enacting antidiscrimination legislation that is tougher than its federal counterpart. New York, for example, has passed a version of the Workplace Religious Freedom Act requiring employers to grant a requested accommodation unless it imposes a significant difficulty or expense.

Working Toward Tolerance

Advocates should capitalize on the widespread criticism of the French proposal by educating elected officials and others about the challenges that confront religious Americans on the job. Instead of battling congressional complacency, advocates should focus their attention on the states in a state-by-state effort to enact strict antidiscrimination laws. Until that happens, employees of faith can take some comfort in the eloquent rebuke that 7th Circuit Judge Frank Easterbrook delivered to Judge Reagan:

> Accommodation of religiously inspired conduct is a token of respect for, and a beacon of welcome to, those whose beliefs differ from the majority's. . . . Obeisance differs from respect; to demand the former in the name of the latter is self-defeating. It is difficult for us to see why a Jew may not wear his yarmulke in court, a Sikh his turban, a Muslim woman her chador, or a Moor his fez . . . [T]hose who keep heads covered as a sign of respect for (or obedience to) a power higher than the state should not be . . . threatened with penalties.

Judge Easterbrook's words of tolerance and respect have resonated among those who have often been forced to choose between their religious and financial obligations. What remains to be seen is whether employers, courts, and legislators will get the message.

"Unless amended, [proposed legislation] would threaten important rights of religious minorities, racial minorities, women, gay men and lesbians, and persons seeking . . . health services."

Laws Protecting Religious Freedom in the Workplace Could Have Harmful Effects

American Civil Liberties Union

A proposed law that would strengthen the requirement that employers accommodate the religious practices of their employees could have negative consequences, argues the American Civil Liberties Union (ACLU) in the following viewpoint. Existing guidelines already help protect workers' religious rights, the ACLU points out. The proposed changes to these guidelines would actually allow workers to discriminate on the basis of stated religious beliefs. The ACLU urges legislators to pass a more narrowly focused law that would avoid undermining basic civil rights.

As you read, consider the following questions:

1. According to the ACLU, what religious accommodation claims might have been decided differently if the Workplace Religious Freedom Act had been law?
2. What kind of changes would the proposed Workplace Religious Freedom Act of 2004 codify into law, according to the ACLU?

The American Civil Liberties Union [ACLU] strongly urges you to oppose S. 893, the Workplace Religious Freedom Act ("WRFA")—unless it is amended to ensure that the legislation will not have the presumably unintended consequence of harming critical personal and civil rights of coworkers, customers, or patients.[1] Unless amended, the bill would threaten important rights of religious minorities, racial minorities, women, gay men and lesbians, and persons seeking reproductive health care and mental health services. . . .

Potential Harm to Civil Rights

Over the past 25 years, employees have brought an array of claims for employers to accommodate religious practices that would have resulted in harm to critical personal or civil rights. If WRFA had been law, the following rejected religious accommodation claims could have been decided differently:

- police officer's request to refuse to protect an abortion clinic,
- another police officer's request to abstain from arresting protestors blocking a clinic entrance,
- social worker's decision to use Bible readings, prayer, and the "casting out of demons" with inmates in a county prison, instead of providing the county's required secular mental health counseling,
- state-employed visiting nurse's decision to tell an AIDS patient and his partner that God "doesn't like the homosexual lifestyle" and that they needed to pray for salvation,
- delivery room nurse's refusal to scrub for an emergency inducement of labor and an emergency caesarian section delivery on women who were in danger of bleeding to death,
- two different male truck drivers and a male emergency medical technician request to avoid overnight work shifts with women because they could not sleep in the same quarters with women,
- employee assistance counselor's request to refuse to counsel unmarried or gay or lesbian employees on relationship issues,

1. As this volume went to press, this bill had not passed into law.

- hotel worker's decision to spray a swastika on a mirror as a religious "good luck" symbol,
- private sector employee's request to uncover and display a KKK tattoo of a hooded figure standing in front of a burning cross,
- state-employed sign language interpreter's request to proselytize and pray aloud for her assigned deaf mental health patients, and
- retail employee's request to begin most statements on the job with "In the name of Jesus Christ of Nazareth."

These examples were all actual cases brought into federal court by employees claiming that their employers refused to provide a reasonable accommodation of their religious beliefs. Applying the existing Title VII reasonable accommodation standard, the courts rejected *all* of these claims. But Congress has no assurance that courts would continue to reject all of these types of claims if WRFA becomes law.

The harm that WRFA could cause is completely avoidable. Congress can—and should—pass legislation tightly focused on strengthening the federal requirements imposed on employers to accommodate workplace scheduling changes for the observation of religious holidays and the wearing of religious clothing or a beard or hairstyle. These two areas of religious accommodation account for nearly three-fourths of all of the religious accommodation claims rejected by federal courts in published opinions during the past quarter-century. A narrowly tailored bill could address these problems for religious minorities without any of the harms that WRFA could cause.

Existing Law Provides a Base Level of Coverage

Title VII of the Civil Rights Act of 1964 requires employers to provide a reasonable accommodation of the religious observance or practice of employees. Although the Supreme Court, in *TWA v. Hardison*, 432 U.S. 63 (1977), limited the employer's obligations under Title VII of the Civil Rights Act of 1964 to accommodate its employees' religious practices at work, employers continue to have a legal duty to accommodate religious exercise in the workplace that does not cause the employer more than a *de minimis* cost.

During the quarter-century after *Hardison*, employees have won about one-third of their litigated claims for scheduling changes for observance of religious holidays, nearly one-half of claims for having a beard or hairstyle for religious reasons, and roughly one-fourth of claims for wearing religious apparel. In addition, employees have won claims for an array of other requested religious accommodations. Of course, these were claims that were actually litigated and resulted in published opinions. Presumably, a large number of additional claims were accommodated by employers without employees having to resort to litigation.

An Overbroad Law

WRFA would broadly strengthen existing requirements imposed on an employer to provide reasonable accommodations of an employee's religious observances and practices in the workplace. Although most of the proponents of WRFA seek only to accommodate the observance of religious holidays and the wearing of beards/hairstyle or religious clothing—and have no interest in harming anyone's rights—WRFA may have a much broader impact than at least most of its supporters intend it to have.

WRFA would make the following three changes in the law:

• Create a definition "*essential functions* of the employment position," but then exempt restrictions on work "practices that may have a *temporary or tangential impact* on the ability to perform job functions" if related to participation in a religious observance or practice (emphasis added);

• Replace the Supreme Court's determination that an employer does not have to provide a reasonable accommodation of a religious practice under Title VII if providing the accommodation would cause anything more than a *de minimis* cost. Instead, an employer can refuse an accommodation only if it would incur "significant difficulty or expense," as determined by factors such as "identifiable cost of the accommodation," the size of the employer, and the location and characteristics of its various facilities; and

• Require that a reasonable accommodation must "remove the conflict between employment requirements and the religious observance or practice of the employee."

The combined effect of these changes will be radically different analyses of those religious accommodation claims that could result in harm to critical personal or civil rights. Congress has no assurance that courts will continue to reject claims that could cause important harm.

Three Possible Problems

First, the introduction of the "essential functions" of the job standard into Title VII's religious accommodation definition raises important questions of which functions of an employee's job are "essential." Increasing numbers of employees will go to court arguing that a refusal to perform all aspects of a job involving health or public safety, unwillingness to comply with employer policies precluding religious or racial harassment, or an objection to sharing overnight work shifts with women do not infringe on any "essential function" of a job. In many cases, an employee would likely bolster his or her claim that a religious practice does not affect an essential function of a job by claiming that the religious practice has nothing more than a *temporary or tangential impact* on the ability to perform job functions," and is thus entirely exempt from the definition of "essential function." Employers will have to determine whether a police officer's decision to pick and choose who he or she is protecting, a medical or mental health worker's decision on who he or she will treat and how the person will be treated, a worker's occasional religious condemnation of a coworker, or the occasional flashing of a swastika or KKK symbol in a "private workplace" is essential or causes nothing more than a temporary or tangential impact on performance. And if the effect on work performance is "temporary or tangential," then the employer will have no choice; it will have to provide the requested accommodation.

Second, WRFA borrows from the Americans with Disabilities Act [ADA] a definition of a "significant difficulty or expense" which would relieve employers of having to provide the requested reasonable accommodation. However, the criteria involve primarily financial factors such as loss of productivity, and the relationship of the costs to the size and structure of the employer. While the definition may be appropriate for a disability rights statute such as the ADA in which the accommodation may require costly changes such as architectural improvements, it has less relevance to a religious antidiscrimination statute. If WRFA passes, employers may have great difficulty defining the "identifiable costs" of allowing employees to proselytize or harass other coworkers or third parties, such as customers or patients. The harmful effect of a particular accommodation on another person might be difficult to express in specifics such as loss of productivity or financial losses relative to the size of the employer.

Not the Responsibility of Employers

Religion, like ballroom dancing or stamp collecting, is a private pursuit and should not be the responsibility of employers. Religion is also inherently divisive—a condition hardly welcomed in today's high-stress work environment. If individuals feel that their religious beliefs will interfere with their ability to perform their jobs, then it is up to them to seek alternative means of employment. That is the American Way.

It should not be the responsibility of an employer to accommodate every religious belief, nor should it be the business of big government to insinuate itself into the daily interactions of individuals in the private workplace.

Ronald Barrier, *CQ Researcher*, August 23, 2002.

Third, the requirement that a reasonable accommodation must "remove the conflict between employment requirements and the religious observance or practice of the employee" would likely bolster arguments that an employer may not simply choose to transfer an employee to another position in order to accommodate an employee. Instead, it could require that employers must change the requirements of the employee's existing position—even when having the employee remain in his or her current position would result in harm to others. Although it is not clear that this "remove the conflict" requirement would necessarily result in employers having to restructure jobs for employees who insist on performing their jobs in ways that harm others, courts will at least have to resolve the question of whether this provision is directed at the specific job of an employee or simply means an equivalent job.

It is impossible to determine the certain effect of WRFA on all possible claims for accommodations that would cause harm, but it is clear that WRFA would be a significant break from how courts decided religious accommodation cases over the past quarter-century. And it is equally clear that the drafters of WRFA have taken no steps to ensure that it could not be used to reverse the outcomes of the types of cases decided during the past 25 years in which an employee was denied a claim to use his or her religious exercise in a way that would harm critical personal or civil rights. . . .

There simply is no reason to create a standard under WRFA that could call into question the resolution of claims such as these requests for accommodations that would result in harm to critical personal or civil rights. Congress can, and should, pass legislation that focuses narrowly on the real problems of scheduling time off for religious holidays and the wearing of religious apparel or a beard. For these reasons, the ACLU urges you to oppose WRFA until amended to avoid any threat of harm to important personal or civil rights.

Periodical Bibliography

The following articles have been selected to supplement the diverse views presented in this chapter.

Dennis Behreandt — "God's Laws and the State," *New American*, September 22, 2003.

Allan C. Brownfeld — "Religion and Public Life: Where Should the Line Be Drawn?" *St. Croix Review*, December 2003.

Edd Doerr — "Jefferson's Wall . . . ," *Humanist*, January/February 2002.

Brian Hansen — "Religion in the Workplace," *CQ Researcher*, August 23, 2002.

Andrew W. Jones — "The War on Religion," *Liberty*, May 2004.

Wendy Kaminer — "The Real Danger Behind the Christian Right: Beware of Conservative Ecumenism," *Free Inquiry*, October/November 2003.

John Leo — "Playing the Bias Card," *U.S. News & World Report*, January 13, 2003.

David Limbaugh — "Removing God from the Public Square," *Human Events*, February 11, 2002.

Michael Newdow — "Why I Did It," *Free Inquiry*, Winter 2002–2003.

Warren A. Nord — "Religion-Free Texts: Getting an Illiberal Education," *Christian Century*, July 14, 1999.

Jeremy Patrick — "Ceremonial Deisms," *Humanist*, January/February 2002.

James Piereson — "'Under God': The History of a Phrase," *Weekly Standard*, October 27, 2003.

Phyllis Schlafly — "We Must Reject the Rule of Judges," *Phyllis Schlafly Report*, March 2004.

Gregory A. Valde — "Schools Without Souls: Moral Community and Public School," *Tikkun*, September 1999.

Emrys Westacott — "Americans Don't Really Believe in the Ten Commandments," *Humanist*, January/February 2004.

Joshua Zatcoff — "The Common Religion of Citizenry," *Freethought Today*, August 2004.

CHAPTER 4

What Values Should Religious Americans Support?

Chapter Preface

In 2003 the Massachusetts Supreme Court ruled that same-sex couples in that state were legally entitled to marry, a decision granting them the same "legal, financial, and social benefits" as heterosexual couples. This unprecedented decision provoked celebration among liberals, gays and lesbians, and their allies, but disquieted social and religious conservatives, as well as some moderates, who believe that the institution of marriage should not be redefined. Echoing conservative sentiments, in 2004 President George W. Bush endorsed a constitutional amendment that would restrict marriage to two people of the opposite sex. "The union of a man and woman is the most enduring human institution, honored and encouraged in all cultures and by every religious faith," Bush explained. "Marriage cannot be severed from its cultural, religious, and natural roots without weakening the good influence of society." The topic of gay marriage seems destined to remain one of the most controversial issues in America, especially among people of faith.

Religious Americans who define themselves as traditionalists generally agree with Bush that marriage serves as the fundamental institution of civilization, promoting the welfare of children and the stability of family and society. Many contend that the marital relationship is rooted in God-given, natural law. "That reproduction of the human race is one of the central purposes of marriage is clear from God's mandate to Adam and Eve . . . to 'be fruitful and increase in number,'" argues Baptist minister Peter Sprigg, who maintains that natural procreation—or at least the potential for procreation—is a central part of the social significance of marriage. Allowing marriage between same-sex couples would, in his opinion, "change the very definition of marriage itself—in effect, [it would define] marriage out of existence. Unless we as Christians (or as Jews, or simply as Americans) speak up, we could lose marriage within the next generation."

Some religious leaders, however, believe that a constitutional amendment banning gay marriage would go too far, in effect legitimizing and sanctioning discriminatory attitudes. Jim Wallis, evangelical minister and editor of *Sojourners* magazine, argues that legalizing civil unions for same-sex couples would provide a "middle way" that is both pro–traditional family and pro–gay and lesbian civil rights: "We can make sure that long-term gay and lesbian partnerships are afforded legitimate legal protections in a pluralistic society without changing our long-standing and deeply rooted concept of marriage as being between a man and a woman. That should continue to be the theology of the church and the way our society best orders itself."

Yet other religious groups disagree with both Sprigg and Wallis and instead publicly affirm a broad, faith-based rationale for supporting full marriage rights for same-sex couples. One such group is the Religious Institute on Sexual Morality, Justice, and Healing, an umbrella organization representing more than ten Christian and Jewish denominations as well as theologians and clergy from diverse religious perspectives. "We refute those who would use selected verses of scripture to condemn the marriage of gay and lesbian people," says Reverend Marvin Ellison, a teacher of Christian social ethics and a member of the Religious Institute. "Contrary to this distortion of religious tradition, the overall message of the Bible neither commends a single marriage model nor commands all to marry, but rather calls for love and justice in all relationships," Ellison asserts.

The widely varying opinions of Sprigg, Wallis, and Ellison show that religious Americans have reached no consensus on issues pertaining to cultural values, such as the definition of marriage. The following chapter provides additional religious perspectives on the subject of marriage as well as other values-laden issues such as social justice, personal morality, abortion, and war.

"Many religious youth and young adults are connecting justice ministry with the need to protect a woman's right to choose safe, legal family planning options."

Religious Americans Should Support the Right to Choose Abortion

Amy Hetrick

Those who uphold the social values of Christianity recognize the importance of a woman's right to reproductive choice, explains Amy Hetrick in the following viewpoint. She claims that a growing number of youths are becoming involved in opportunities that connect their religious faith with pro-choice activism. Some, for example, travel to abortion clinics to serve as a peaceful pro-choice presence during antiabortion demonstrations, writes Hetrick. The author applauds the efforts of religious groups that encourage youths to have an impact on reproductive choice issues in their communities. Hetrick is the Youth Initiative coordinator for the Religious Coalition for Reproductive Choice.

As you read, consider the following questions:
1. How did Amy Hetrick's spiritual journey begin?
2. What is the Religious Coalition for Reproductive Choice, according to Hetrick?
3. In what way did Sarah Kurien's participation in a Peaceful Presence action strengthen her faith, according to the author?

Amy Hetrick, "Prayerfully Pro-Choice," *Christian Social Action*, vol. 15, May/June 2002, pp. 9–12. Copyright © 2002 by *Christian Social Action*. Reproduced by permission.

B ishop Melvin G. Talbert, former bishop of The United Methodist Church in the San Francisco area, once said, "To be for choice is to be willing to enter into the pain and the struggle of life in the real world, and in the face of that reality, to choose. It is in this context that we are challenged to face the ambiguity and the complexity of conflicting values and judgment. Our faith compels us to respect others' values, life circumstances and decisions."

Many religious youth and young adults are connecting justice ministry with the need to protect a woman's right to choose safe, legal family planning options.

The Social Values of Christianity

I am a 27-year-old middle-class white woman and have identified as a religious person for only a few years. As a youth, I was unable to see religion as a positive force in the world. My spiritual journey was not able to begin until I learned that many religious people feel a moral and religious imperative to work for the same social justice causes about which I feel so passionately including anti-racism, the environment, human rights, and yes, reproductive choice.

I began to open myself up to learning more about the religiously-based compassionate social values of Christianity and consequently grew deeply in my faith. A few years later I enthusiastically accepted the Youth Initiative Coordinator position at the Religious Coalition for Reproductive Choice. I wanted the opportunity not only to help other young people find peace in being both religious and pro-choice, but also to provide them with opportunities to put their faith into action to safeguard the future of choice.

Spiritual Youth for Reproductive Freedom

The Religious Coalition for Reproductive Choice began in 1973 and is a national, interfaith organization of 40 religiously and theologically diverse groups, including two agencies of The United Methodist Church. By 1999, the youngest Religious Coalition activists became increasingly aware that even they were beyond their reproductive years and that there were no new, young religious activists joining them to work for choice. The Coalition decided that it needed to reach out to and train a younger generation of pro-faith, pro-choice activists—a generation that would be empowered to advocate for its own reproductive rights and carry on the struggle of its parents' and grandparents' generation to keep abortion safe and legal.

The Bible and Abortion

Jesus never mentioned abortion or sanctity of life. Nowhere in the Scriptures is there any reference to sacredness or sanctity or respect for fetal life. The only reference that comes close to this is Luke 2:23: "Every male that opens the womb shall be called holy to the Lord." It is characteristic of both Jewish and Christian Scripture that one must be born to be respected or to participate in the holy. . . .

Although abortion was widely practiced in the ancient world, there is not one reference against abortion in the entire New Testament. Even in the Hebrew Scripture, or Old Testament, the only reference to individual abortion is in Numbers 5, where God commanded an abortion with respect to an unfaithful wife. Elsewhere God is quoted as having ordered many hundreds of abortions. In Isaiah 13 and Hosea 13 there are references to "ripping up women with child" and destroying "the fruit of the womb."

John M. Swomley, *Human Quest*, March/April 1999.

In the fall of 2000, the Religious Coalition launched a Youth Initiative to educate, organize, and empower young people between the ages of 16–30 to become the next generation of pro-faith, pro-choice leaders. Early in its first year, the Youth Initiative was named Spiritual Youth for Reproductive Freedom (SYRF) and established an interfaith Youth Advisory Committee that includes two United Methodists—a young adult leader and a young minister—who work with religious youth. In recent months we have developed an interactive website, www.syrf.org, and we have begun to form SYRF groups on campuses and in congregations.

The youth and young adult response to SYRF has been wonderful! The Religious Coalition has discovered that when given the forum and the opportunity, youth and young adults not only care about reproductive choice issues, but many are enthusiastically getting involved in SYRF's work and finding it to be incredibly satisfying.

Sarah's Story

Sarah Kurien, a fabulous young woman and an intern with The United Methodist Church's General Board of Church and Society's Ethnic Young Adult summer internship program, describes her placement with the Religious Coalition for Reproductive Choice as a very rewarding experience. When Sarah began her internship, she already thought of abortion (in her words) "as a woman's right with choice as a God-given right that no one can take away." Sarah knew what The United Methodist Social Principles said on the topic of reproductive choice, but admits she did not think very much about the issue before her placement with the Religious Coalition. She says that she sought out the internship so that she could learn how United Methodist theological principles apply to the pursuit of social justice.

"Faith motivates me to work for justice. I serve God by serving men and women. Getting involved in the internship was the next step in my faith journey." Sarah says that her placement with the Religious Coalition's Youth Initiative provided that opportunity and so much more. Her internship helped her grow in her faith because she had the chance to ask questions, challenge herself, and strengthen her faith.

Peaceful Presence

One experience in particular led to this transformation—when she traveled with the Religious Coalition to an abortion clinic in Wichita, Kansas to be part of a pro-choice *Peaceful Presence* while anti-choice demonstrators picketed the clinic and attempted to shut it down. This is how Sarah recalls that experience:

"Being in Wichita for Peaceful Presence was the most intense and challenging faith experience of my life. I knew their songs [the religious songs of the anti-choice demonstrators]. They looked like people in my church. The passages they read were ones I had grown up reciting. And yet the God they claimed to be theirs was so different from the God I knew. They preached about God's judgment, but not the God of justice and unconditional love that allows us to make choices. They were yelling, shoving graphic pictures in our faces, while we stood silently and peacefully as a religious pro-choice presence. I was there to empower those women who entered the clinic—to let them know that not all religious people condemn them for making the difficult decision to have an abortion.

"Ironically, I understood that the anti-choice demonstrators were there to fight for justice too. The situation proposed two very opposing views of God and justice. I had to ask myself questions to understand the differences, including what is justice to God? How am I called to fight for justice? What role can I play in serving a just God; am I right, am I wrong, and how am I supposed to know?

"At one particular moment, I was able to derive some sort of answer to these questions. The other demonstrators were playing a very popular contemporary Christian song, and I felt so alone and vulnerable. I took a deep breath, to help clear my mind from the perplexities running through my head. One of the other pro-choice supporters touched my back. At that moment, I felt such an amazing connection to him, and to God. I felt so empowered! God was telling me to do this, and He was with me. He told me to hold my sign up high. I lifted the sign, and I held my head up high and smiled. I felt an amazing and rejuvenating spiritual strength. I knew that the issue was much greater than here and now—and that there is so much more to work for. From that single experience, I took 10 giant leaps in my faith journey. I learned that I have the God-given power to do so much good in the world."

Working for Choice

Of course, not every young person who gets involved in SYRF has the opportunity to take part in a pro-choice Peaceful Presence as intense as the one in Wichita [in the summer of 2001]. SYRF does, however, provide youth and young adults with a safe, open, and affirming forum to ask challenging theological questions about faith and justice, the resources and support to help them grow in their faith commitment to social justice, and the opportunity to be heard and make a difference in reproductive choice issues in their communities.

SYRF is providing youth and young adults with the opportunity to experience perhaps for the first time the spirit of Bishop Talbert's wisdom. This theology is being lived out through the pro-choice social action experiences of Sarah Kurien in Wichita and through the work of other SYRF young people in other communities in this country. It is this opportunity to connect theology of choice with the commitment to work for social justice that SYRF is offering our next generation of pro-faith, pro-choice leaders.

"The Church has a responsibility . . . to provide a solution to the abortion problem in America and the world."

Religious Americans Should Reject Abortion

Concerned Women for America

Unrestricted abortion has cheapened the value of human life and has had far-reaching negative effects on American society, argues Concerned Women for America (CWA) in the following viewpoint. According to CWA, easy access to abortion kills innocent life, damages relationships between men and women, and creates an environment in which other infractions against life—such as infanticide and euthanasia—are more acceptable. While the church should openly oppose abortion, it has failed to come to a consensus on the issue. In keeping with biblical principles and with the ideals of the Founding Fathers, Americans of faith should support the right to life. Concerned Women for America is a national advocacy organization that supports traditional Judeo-Christian values.

As you read, consider the following questions:
1. According to Jeff Jacoby, as quoted by CWA, how has abortion affected male-female relationships?
2. In what cases can parents sue their doctors for "wrongful birth," according to the author?
3. According to Francis Schaeffer, as quoted by CWA, what kind of churches take public stands against abortion?

After [more than] 30 years, abortion has had a phenomenal impact on society. "Decriminalized" abortion has liberated women, advocates argue. But are they really better off because of the U.S. Supreme Court *Roe v. Wade* decision [legalizing abortion]? And how has abortion affected the lives of men? Actually, unrestricted abortion has cheapened human life, thus affecting all aspects of American society.

Impact on Women

Advocates claimed abortion would bring women "freedom" and "empowerment." Sadly, the opposite has occurred. Instead of freeing women from male exploitation, abortion has made them more vulnerable—playing into the hands of men who seek sex without marriage.

Columnist Jeff Jacoby discusses abortion's impact on male-female relationships:

> It has corrupted romance and sexuality. In the ancient times before *Roe*, the price of an unwanted pregnancy could be terrifyingly high. That gave unmarried women a powerful incentive to be careful—to reserve themselves for men whom they knew to be worthy. Sometimes worthiness could be proven only by walking down a church aisle; if not that, it often required at least courtship, love and commitment.

> But after *Roe*, an unwanted pregnancy became little more then a nuisance. To undo it, you had only to see an abortionist. So why be careful? Why hold back? There was no longer a need to wait for that aisle walk—or even for commitment. . . . For men who wanted sex without strings, without having to make promises, without having to go through the rituals of romance, *Roe* was a godsend. And if she has a baby? Hey, that's her problem. She could have gotten an abortion.

In the past, fear and respect have motivated people to make responsible sexual choices. But since *Roe* divided sex from reproduction, people stopped being responsible for the consequences of their actions. Exercising so-called "equality," women began engaging in sex with little discretion. When women inevitably became pregnant, abortionists were waiting.

Impact on Men

While abortion has degraded women, it has also negatively influenced men. Some laugh at the idea of men being "victims" of abortion. But counselor and author Steve Arterburn understands the psychological conflict and its ramifications. He pressured his girlfriend into having an abortion after getting her pregnant during his first year of college.

"I had selfishly destroyed a human life because I didn't want to be inconvenienced," he explained. "I'm one of the thousands of abortion fathers who have also gone through this ordeal. In my case, it resulted in 80 ulcers eating at my stomach, intestines and colon. The pain was excruciating and made worse by the knowledge that it was a result of my secret sin."

Just as abortion demands that women violate their natural inclination to nurture, it forces men to reject their role as provider and protector. The new life should motivate the man to embrace new levels of responsibility. Instead, he acts against his instincts, destroying what he should most vehemently defend—his own child. . . .

Far-Reaching Effects

Initially, abortion-on-demand cheapened the life of the unborn child, but the downslide did not stop there. *Roe v. Wade* placed America on the edge of a slippery slope. And one does not have to be an expert to see how far we've fallen since 1973.

For some, abortion has become simply a form of birth control. Theresa Flores is not sure how many abortions she has had—she thinks nine. After her first abortion around the age of 15, she continued having unprotected sex with her boyfriend. Over the next few years, the abortions continued. "I basically used abortion as a form of birth control," she admitted.

In 1973, Dr. Francis Shaeffer predicted that abortion would be the first step in a downward spiral:

> Of all the subjects relating to the erosion of the sanctity of human life, abortion is the keystone. It is the first and crucial issue that has been overwhelming in changing attitudes toward the value of life in general . . . Since life is being destroyed before birth, why not tamper with it on the other end? Will a society which has assumed the right to kill infants in the womb . . . have difficulty in assuming the right to kill other human beings?

By the time the peak of the baby boom reaches retirement age, the number of abortions since *Roe v. Wade* will equal the number of births in the baby boom.

One only needs to look at recent headlines to see how Schaeffer's prediction has come true: From the advancement of the "Right to Die" movement to Princeton bioethicist Peter Singer, who openly advocates infanticide up to 28 days after birth. "Killing a defective infant is not morally equivalent to killing a person," Singer argued in his 1979 book *Practical Ethics*. "Sometimes it is not wrong at all."

The False Religion of "Choice"

G.K. Chesterton observed that those not believing in God are ready to believe in anything. Similarly, one could observe that those rejecting the teachings of traditional religion are ready to make a religion out of anything. For pro-abortionists, "choice" is their religion (They even speak of abortion as a "rite of passage," an "empowering" experience. Some of the more extreme adherents of the religion of "choice" even consider abortion a kind of sacrament.)

The primitive religion of "choice" has no substantive underpinnings: neither in science nor the laws of nature, neither in sound moral theology nor in divine revelation. Its appeal lies in its promise of a moral shortcut, a quick way out of a difficult situation. "Her God" gives a woman permission to act out of narrow self-interest and for the sake of convenience: "Let's get it over with and go on." The moral shortcut, however, comes at a heavy price: Not only is an innocent child dead, but those who robbed that unborn child of its personhood, logically, declared themselves worthless.

Wanda Franz, *National Right to Life News*, January 22, 1999.

Today, if their child is born with a congenital defect, parents in some states can sue their doctor for "wrongful birth" if he does not recommend abortion. For example, in New Jersey, Deborah Campano and her now ex-husband Michael Imbergamo won a suit against Dr. James Delahunty, to the tune of $1.85 million. Campano said she would have aborted her son Michael if she knew he had Down syndrome.

"What we're dealing with here is the promotion of eugenics as a birth policy whereby doctors are sued for not weeding out the 'unfit,'" said Clark Forsythe, president of Americans United for Life. . . .

Now, the mentality that life does not inherently have value

has reached into the lives of other vulnerable members of our society. As health care costs rise, the elderly have become targets. They find themselves pressured to accept euthanasia so they will not be too much of a "burden" on society.

An Abandoned Generation

"[T]here is another group of children who have been overlooked in the [abortion] debate . . . the children now 10 or 15 or even 20 years old who have had it drummed into them by TV, radio and magazines," writes Peggy Noonan, former speechwriter for President [Ronald] Reagan and author of *What I Saw at the Revolution* and *The Case Against Hillary.* "Is it too much to see a connection between the abortion culture in which these young people came of age and the moral dullness they are accused of displaying?"

This disrespect for life has had a profound effect on teens: Melissa Drexler was a teenager who managed to hide her pregnancy to full term. She gave birth in a toilet stall and then allegedly choked or suffocated her 6-lb., 6-oz. son. Minutes later, she returned to the floor of her high school formal dance in Aberdeen Township, New Jersey, where she ate salad and danced with her boyfriend.

The epidemic of baby abandonment, or "dumping," is growing. According to the Department of Health and Human Services (HHS), the number of babies found abandoned in public places increased from 65 to 105 between 1991 and 1998. Of those, eight were found dead in 1991, and 33 were found dead in 1998. Further, the number of children abandoned at hospitals grew from 22,000 in 1991 to more than 31,000 in 1998. During this same time period, teenage pregnancies and abortions were both *dropping.* Maureen Hogan, president of Adopt America, blames the pervasive "just-get-rid-of-it mentality."

As a result of this epidemic, many ministries have blossomed:

• In Pittsburgh, Pennsylvania, Gigi Kelly started Baskets for Babies. Volunteer families avail themselves to desperate women who can leave their babies literally on their doorsteps. Now 608 families leave their porch lights lit, with baskets waiting.

• In Houston, Texas, billboards—including a hotline, 1-800-904-SAVE—plead "Don't Abandon Your Baby!" The signs urge women to leave their babies at fire stations or hospitals.

• In Mobile, Alabama, after a rash of baby dumpings, television reporter Jodie Brooks met with social workers and hospital administrators. They started A Secret Safe Place for Newborns.

• In Yucaipa, California, Debi Faris started the Garden of Angels in 1996, a cemetery for dead abandoned babies. She names the infants and gives them decent burials. . . .

The Church's Response

Undoubtedly, abortion grieves the heart of God. Considering this, the church should be abortion's most vocal opponent. However, the church has been unable to reach a consensus on this issue.

Even in the years leading up to *Roe*, the church was in conflict. Surprisingly, some clergy even helped lead pro-abortion forces in the 1960s. The Clergy Consultation Service on Abortion in New York helped 100,000 women receive abortions before they were legal.

Theologian and philosopher Dr. Francis Schaeffer writes:

> In general, the denominations which hold to the historical Bible-believing position have taken a public stand against abortion. If you are in a denomination which supports abortion, consider what is your responsibility. . . . [Y]our name is being used to support a low view of human life.

Simply condemning abortion is not enough. The Church has a responsibility to show the love of Christ to these women who are in desperate situations, and therefore, it is uniquely positioned to provide a solution to the abortion problem in America and the world.

Many churches have established and/or supported pregnancy resource centers (PRCs) within their communities. About 3,000 operate nationwide. Some provide counseling within the church itself and even help provide every form of assistance and support women need, from the physical and financial to the emotional and spiritual. . . .

Churches on Abortion

While the views of individual pastors and congregations vary, most denominations have adopted formal positions on abortion.

• Roman Catholic Church—Vatican II's "Church in the Modern World" held in 1965 that "life must be protected with the utmost care from the moment of conception: Abortion and infanticide are unspeakable crimes."

• Episcopal Church—A 1994 resolution expressed "unequivocal opposition" to actions that "abridge the right of a woman to reach an informed decision about the termination of her pregnancy" or that "limit access" to safe abortions.

• Evangelical Lutheran Church in America—In 1990, the church accepted abortion as a "last resort" in cases of extreme fetal abnormality, rape, incest or threat to the mother's life. Otherwise, the church "neither supports nor opposes" laws against abortion.

• Lutheran Church-Missouri Synod—The Missouri synod has "consistently taken a strong position in support of human life and in opposition to willful abortion."

• Southern Baptist Convention—In 1976, Southern Baptists opposed abortion as a means of birth control and in 1980 backed anti-abortion legislation and a constitutional amendment to protect life from the moment of conception.

• American Baptist Churches—In 1994, the denomination said it "acknowledges diversity" among members but took no official stand.

• United Methodist Church—The 1996 "Book of Discipline" supports abortion rights, but adds words on the "sanctity of unborn life" and rejects abortion as a "means of birth control [or] gender selection."

• United Church of Christ—The church has strongly supported legal abortion since 1971. It opposed the 1996 partial-birth abortion ban and supports federal funding for abortion in all health legislation.

• Presbyterian Church (USA)—The church has accepted "personal choice" in abortion, but in 1992, added that tradition also provides a basis for the "preservation of the lives of the unborn." In 1997, the church expressed "grave moral concern" over partial-birth abortion.

- Presbyterian Church in America (PCA)—Respecting the sanctity of human life, PCA defines abortion as the intentional killing of an unborn child and upholds that Scripture affirms the personhood of the unborn; thus, the Sixth Commandment prohibits the shedding of innocent blood.
- Orthodox churches—The Orthodox Christian denominations oppose abortion and support restrictive legislation.
- Mennonite Church—It recognizes that "abortion violates the Biblical principles of the sanctity and value of human life," yet does not desire to "legislate morality for society."

Smear Campaigns

Sadly, CPCs [crisis pregnancy centers] come under attack from pro-abortionists. In 1999, when support for CPCs grew among legislators and presidential candidates, the National Abortion and Reproductive Rights Action League (NARAL) resurrected a smear campaign against CPCs. NARAL claimed the clinics lied about providing medical services. However, many CPCs are medical clinics.

For example, Choices Medical Clinic in Wichita, Kansas —next to the infamous abortionist George Tiller—offers physician examinations, pregnancy testing and obstetrician ultrasound examinations.

Opponents also claim PRCs lie to women. One "lie," they say, is that a woman's intestines can be sucked out during an abortion. But that is not a lie. California abortionist Bruce Steir pleaded guilty to manslaughter for killing a patient when he punctured her uterus and pulled her intestine through the hole. Despite opposition, PRCs continue to meet women's real needs with compassion.

Looking Ahead

Our Founding Fathers created a nation based on life, liberty and the pursuit of happiness. "Switch the order of these three fundamental human rights—Putting happiness before liberty or liberty before life—and you end up with moral chaos and social anarchy," wrote Steve Forbes, successful businessman and former U.S. presidential candidate.

Americans must ask: Do we wish to leave the abortion mentality to future generations? Is our country better off because of *Roe*? Today America stands at a crossroad. The choice is clear. God extolled the Israelites: "I have set before you life and death, blessing and cursing; therefore choose life, that both you and your descendants may live" (Deuteronomy 30: 19, NKJV). The time has come to choose life—for the unborn and also for our entire society.

"We call on religious and civic leaders to promote good marriages . . . without restrictions based on the biological sex, procreative potential, or sexual orientation of the partners."

Religious Leaders Should Support Same-Sex Marriage

Religious Institute on Sexual Morality, Justice, and Healing

In the following viewpoint the Religious Institute on Sexual Morality, Justice, and Healing asserts that there are religious foundations for supporting the marriage of same-sex couples. Sexuality—including sexual orientation—is a God-given gift that should be affirmed, the authors contend. Since all humans are created for relationship, the authors argue, they should all have the right to express their love, commitment, and faithfulness through marriage regardless of sexual orientation. Moreover, the Bible's overriding message of love, justice, and inclusion of outcasts should encourage religious leaders to promote marriage rights for all. This viewpoint is excerpted from an open letter that was written at a multifaith colloquium of theologians sponsored by the Religious Institute.

As you read, consider the following questions:

1. In the authors' opinion, why should religious leaders avoid relying solely on scripture for understanding marriage in the modern world?
2. Which religious denominations perform union ceremonies for same-sex couples, according to the authors?

A s religious leaders, we are committed to promoting the well-being and moral and spiritual integrity of persons and society. Today, we are called to join the public discussion about marriage equality. There are strong civil liberties arguments for ending the exclusion of same-sex couples from the legal institution of marriage. Here we invite you to consider *religious foundations* for securing the freedom to marry for same-sex couples. Marriage equality is about more than gaining equal access to the legal protections and responsibilities of marriage. It raises fundamental questions about justice and power, intimate relationships, sexuality and gender, respect for diverse families, and the role of religion as well as the state in these matters.

A Life-Giving Gift

Our religious traditions celebrate that humans are created in and for relationship and that sexuality is God's life-giving and life-fulfilling gift. We affirm the dignity and worth of all persons and recognize sexual difference as a blessed part of our endowment. There can be no justification for discrimination on the basis of sexual orientation or gender identity. As religious leaders, we believe that *all* persons have the right to lead lives that express love, justice, mutuality, commitment, consent and pleasure, including but not limited to civil and religious marriage.

Affirming Marriage and Family

From a religious perspective, marriage is about entering into a holy covenant and making a commitment with another person to share life's joys and sorrows. Marriage is valued because it creates stable, committed relationships; provides a means to share economic resources; and nurtures the individual, the couple, and children. Good marriages benefit the community and express the religious values of long-term commitment, generativity, and faithfulness. In terms of these religious values, there is no difference in marriages between a man and a woman, two men, or two women. Moreover, as our traditions affirm, where there is love, the sacred is in our midst.

Marriage is an evolving civil and religious institution. In the past, marriage was primarily about property and procreation whereas today the emphasis is on egalitarian partnership, companionship, and love. In the past, neither the state nor most religions recognized divorce and remarriage, interracial marriage, or the equality of the marriage partners. These understandings changed, and rightly so, in greater recognition of the humanity of persons and their moral and civil rights. Today, we are called to embrace another change, this time the freedom of same-sex couples to marry.

Scripture and Tradition

The biblical call to justice and compassion (love neighbor as self) provides the mandate for marriage equality. Justice as right relationship seeks both personal and communal well-being. It is embodied in interpersonal relationships and institutional structures, including marriage. Justice seeks to eliminate marginalization for reasons of race, gender, sexual orientation, or economic status.

We find support for marriage equality in scripture and tradition in their overriding messages about love, justice, and inclusion of the marginalized. Even so, we cannot rely exclusively on scripture for understanding marriage today. For example, biblical texts that encourage celibacy, forbid divorce, or require women to be subservient to their husbands are no longer authoritative. At the same time, there are also many biblical models for blessed relationships beyond one man and one woman. Indeed, scripture neither commends a single marriage model nor commands all to marry, but rather calls for love and justice in all relationships.

Marriage Equality Supports Strong Families

In our nation, families take many forms. All families should be supported in building stable, empowering, and respectful relationships. Marriage equality is a means to strengthen families and is especially beneficial to children raised by same-sex couples. The state should not deny same-sex couples access to civil marriage. Many such couples are in long-term committed relationships and yet remain without legal and, in many cases, religious recognition. Conversely, because the emotional and spiritual bond of marriage is precious, the state should not compel anyone to marry (e.g., in

Mill. © by Mill Newsart Syndicate. Reproduced by permission.

order to qualify for public assistance).

The United States is one of the most diverse religious countries in the world. No single religious voice can speak for all traditions on issues of sexuality and marriage, nor should government take sides on religious differences. Therefore, religious groups must have the right to discern who is eligible for marriage in their own tradition. In addition, all clergy should be free to solemnize marriages without state interference. We also note that many religious traditions already perform marriages and unions for same-sex couples. We call on the state neither to recognize only certain religious marriages as legal nor to penalize those who choose not to marry. The benefits and protections offered by the state to individuals and families should be available according to need, not marital status. The best way to protect our nation's precious religious freedom is to respect the separation of church and state when it comes to equality under the law.

We call on religious and civic leaders to promote good marriages based on responsibility, equity, and love, without restrictions based on the biological sex, procreative potential, or sexual orientation of the partners.

Good marriages:
- are committed to the mutual care and fulfillment of both partners
- increase the capacity of the individuals to contribute to the common good
- assure that all children are wanted, loved, and nurtured
- are free of threats, violence, exploitation, and intimidation.

The faiths we affirm challenge us to speak and act for justice for all who seek to express their love in the commitment of marriage. Some people of faith differ with us; others may be undecided. To each and all, we reach out and seek to promote what is best for individuals, couples, families, children, and society. Our commitment is not only for the legal rights of some, but relational justice for all.

Religious Support for Marriage Equality

Many denominations are considering their policies on holy unions and the legal right to marry. As of fall 2004:

- Several religious denominations have endorsed their clergy performing commitment or union ceremonies for same-sex couples. These include the Central Conference of American Rabbis (Reform Judaism), the Ecumenical Catholic Church, Ohalah, Alliance for Jewish Renewal, the Reconstructionist Rabbinical Association, the Unitarian Universalist Association and the Universal Fellowship of Metropolitan Community Churches.

- The United Church of Christ, the American Baptist Churches, the Christian Church (Disciples of Christ), and various Quaker groups leave the decision to perform same-sex unions to their clergy, congregations, or local governing bodies. The Presbyterian Church (USA) and the Episcopal Church in the United States of America allow their clergy to bless same-sex unions, if their clergy do not call them marriage.

- Several denominations have endorsed the rights of same-sex couples to legally marry and/or opposed federal and state efforts to deny marriage equality.
- In 1996, the Unitarian Universalist Association passed a resolution in support of marriage equality. The same year, the Central Conference of American Rabbis passed a resolution supporting the "right of gay and lesbian couples to share fully and equally in the rights of civil marriage." The Executive Council of the United Church of Christ in April 2004 affirmed "equal rights for all couples who seek to have their relationships recognized by the state." Other religious organizations that either support civil marriage for same-sex couples and/or who are on record opposing the denial of equal rights to same-sex couples include the American Friends Service Committee, Dignity USA, Ecumenical Catholic Church, Interfaith Working Group, Presbyterian Church (USA), Reconstructionist Rabbinical Association, and the Universal Fellowship of Metropolitan Churches.
- More than 2250 religious leaders have endorsed the Religious Declaration on Sexual Morality, Justice, and Healing, which calls for full inclusion of sexual minorities, including their ordination and performance of same-sex unions.
- More than 4000 religious leaders have endorsed the marriage resolution sponsored by Freedom to Marry.

"This is the beautiful biblical picture: a two-gendered, complementary couple improving on and channeling nature, but neither conquering it nor twisting it."

Religious Leaders Should Support Traditional Marriage

David Neff

Local churches must lead the way in reviving the traditional definition of marriage, argues David Neff in the following viewpoint. This traditional definition, rooted in biblical understanding, reveals marriage to be a loving, committed, faithful, and procreative relationship between one man and one woman, Neff contends. Legalizing same-sex unions undermines marriage because it goes against nature and reinforces the misguided notion that marriage is simply a form of individual self-fulfillment and sexual expression. True marriage is not a form of expressive individualism, Neff writes; it is instead a biblically defined relationship rooted in loyalty, service, and sacrifice—a union that provides a foundation for community and society. Neff is editor of *Christianity Today*, a monthly magazine of evangelical Christian opinion.

As you read, consider the following questions:

1. In Neff's opinion, what does the church need to repent for as it works to reestablish traditional marriage?
2. How might male-female relationships be affected if same-sex marriage became common, according to authorities quoted by Neff?

David Neff, "A Marriage Revolution: By Practicing What We Believe, Christian Marriage Can Transform Our Society," *Marriage Partnership*, vol. 21, Spring 2004. Copyright © 2003 by Christianity Today, Inc. Reproduced by permission of the author.

Same-sex marriage makes perfect sense—if you buy North American culture's take on sex and marriage. More than four decades after the introduction of the Pill, hardly anyone now getting married remembers the time when pleasure, procreation, passion, companionship, and parenthood were all intimately knotted into a bundle called marriage. Without those connections, marriage has become an arena for mere self-fulfillment and sexual expression. Even the Ontario Court, in its June 10, 2003, affirmation of same-sex marriage, could describe marriage as only an expression of love and commitment. If that's all there is to marriage, why not grant the same legal benefits to committed same-sex couples as to married heterosexuals?

There is, however, an alternative view, rooted in the Bible, in history, in tradition, and in nature. And those of us who see marriage through those lenses can only think of "same-sex marriage" as we think of "fat-free sour cream"—a triumph of the modern, technologically blunted imagination.

The modern spirit has often been devoted to overcoming nature with technology. This has been a blessing when it has nearly wiped out some life-threatening diseases. Unfortunately, it's also synthesized inferior substitutes for real things, ranging from the invention of calorie-free sweeteners to the recent creation of embryos that were genetically both male and female.

That same modernist spirit is at work in the juggernaut that seems bent on normalizing same-sex marriage. May God bless the resistance: Matt Daniels and the Alliance for Marriage for promoting the Federal Marriage Amendment [although the amendment has not yet been approved]. Rep. Marilyn Musgrave (R-Colo.) and her 75 colleagues cosponsoring the Amendment in Congress. And Maggie Gallagher for elucidating the cultural consequence of legalizing same-sex marriage.

A Laboratory for Marriage

Still, the local church has a key role in re-creating a biblical understanding of marriage in our society.

First, we must admit that the church's current record is dismal. Divorce statistics inside the church are indistinguishable from those outside.

Second, we need to repent for allowing our culture's blind abandon toward expressive individualism to permeate the way many of our churches relate to marriage, divorce, and remarriage.

Third, we need to restore the community context of marriage. A married couple is more than the sum of its parts. It's a thread in a community fabric. Societies are built out of people who are loyal to one another and who work and sacrifice for the common good. Expressive individualism is a poor foundation for a society, and marriages so conceived don't build loyalties or give us practice in sacrificial service. Marriages and families should be schools for service.

Fourth, we need to recover the sense of human limitation inherent in marriage and family life. This is the beautiful biblical picture: a two-gendered, complementary couple improving on and channeling nature, but neither conquering it nor twisting it.

Living with Nature

Modernism is about conquering nature, but marriage is about living with nature. Illness and irritating habits, economic reverses and recalcitrant children—these things give us practice in living with limits. *Sing Me to Heaven* is Margaret Kim Peterson's affecting memoir of building a marriage in the face of limitations. Knowing that her husband had a terminal illness from the beginning helped her realize that marriage isn't choosing a future; it's choosing a partner with whom to face the future. And to varying degrees, that always involves living with limits as "helpers suitable for each other."

Fifth, churches must help their members recover the link between marriage and procreation. In the 1970s, the evangelical subculture rightly affirmed the delights of marital sex through popular books such as *The Total Woman* and *Intended for Pleasure*. ("Fundies in their undies!" joked church historian Martin Marty in response.) Unfortunately, even in the church, the procreative dimension of sex has been sidelined by economic pressures, cultural ideals, and technological fixes. Churches need to celebrate the fact that every marriage is procreative by design.

Sixth, churches must continue to help their members learn the practical skills associated with all of the challenges of married life. There is no lack of resources: organizations such as Marriage Savers and Marriage Encounter, cautionary studies such as Judith Wallerstein's *The Unexpected Legacy of Divorce*, and inspirations such as Mike Mason's classic *Mystery of Marriage*. While resources abound, focus is needed. The restoration of Christian marriage should be at the top of our congregational agendas.

The Big Yellow Taxi Factor

A favorite anthem of early '70s counterculture was Joni Mitchell's "Big Yellow Taxi." In a familiar refrain, she mourned the passing of unspoiled nature: "Don't it always seem to go that you don't know what you've got till it's gone? They paved paradise and put up a parking lot."

When the states passed a rash of no-fault divorce laws in the '60s and '70s, few anticipated the disastrous impact on the economic and psychological well-being of women and children. When same-sex marriage is legalized, the unanticipated cultural impact and personal costs may likewise be enormous.

Cosmological Rebellion

In seeking to remove the divinely ordained natural sexual distinction, we have moved beyond perversion to cosmological rebellion. Perversion distorts what is natural, even while it presupposes it. Homosexual activists now seeking to avail themselves of the name and benefits of monogamous marriage presuppose that marriage is a permanent and exclusive union between two human beings, but that framework itself emerges from the truth that the sexual union of one male and one female produces a quite permanent and indissoluble living union, a child. Circumvent the sexual necessity for male and female to make a child, and blur, smear, and stir male and female like so much paint, and marriage as a moral structure will simply decay through disuse. Behold, the end of marriage —even the perverted form of homosexual marriage.

Benjamin D. Wiker, *Crisis*, July/August 2004.

The truth about marriage is embedded in nature, and nature has a way of reasserting itself. Inevitably, the Big Yellow

Taxi factor will come into play: People will long for what once was. The challenge to the church is to be a countercultural outpost, modeling marriage as it should be for the world. Those with an impoverished understanding of marriage will be able to grasp it only when they see the real thing.

It's time to start the revolution.

Questions and Answers

Q. Why is marriage between a man and a woman better than the alternatives?

A. "The sexual union of a man and a woman in the context of marriage has the potential of producing children and continuing the human race. Sexual union between two people of the same sex doesn't hold this potential."

—Gary D. Chapman, Ph.D., author of *The Five Love Languages*

"Aside from the obvious answer (that's the way God made it), marriage between a man and a woman is better because marriage is meant, in part, to reflect or reveal the nature of God, and sameness isn't what we see in the Trinity. In the Trinity we see equality in essence coupled with diversity in role. God teaches us of himself when he teaches us to love and relish our differences, including the differences between sexes."

—Elyse Fitz, author of *Helper by Design*

"Marriage between a man and a woman reflects and complements God's own personality. God made males and females as two distinct parts of himself. Gender differences reflect the kaleidoscope of God's characteristics. No other types of "marriage" can show the diversity of God like the loving male/female one does."

—Shay Roop, Ph.D., pyschotherapist, sex therapist, and author of *For Women Only: God's Design for Female Sexuality and Intimacy*

Q. How would the long-term health of male/female marriages be affected if same-sex marriages become commonplace?

A. "Two comes from two genders, male and female. From the beginning, it has been so. Now that this foundation has been deconstructed as unnecessary, does the binary nature of marriage . . . matter that much? If husband and wife are not sacred and worth preserving, then why is 'two' sacred?"

—Warren Throckmorton, director of College Counseling and an associate professor of psychology at Grove City College.

"Same-sex marriage will be a public and legal declaration that . . . children do not need mothers and fathers. Alternative family forms are not only just as good, they are just the same as a husband and wife raising kids together. . . .

"Marriage is our most basic social institution for protecting children. Same-sex marriage amounts to a vast social experiment on children. Rewriting the basic rules of marriage puts all children, not just the children in unisex unions, at risk. Do not expect boys to become good family men in a society [that] believes, as they have been taught, that men are optional in family life."

—Maggie Gallagher, from Marriagedebate.com

"We [must] become prophetic people and say that war is never blessed by God and you cannot follow Jesus by supporting war no matter what the president wants to tell us."

Christians Should Embrace Nonviolence

John Dear, interviewed by Stephen Morris

John Dear is a Jesuit priest, writer, and peace activist who has been arrested dozens of times in acts of civil disobedience. In the following viewpoint Dear maintains that Christianity is essentially nonviolent because Jesus's basic teachings emphasized compassion and love of one's enemies. Christians should therefore reject war and resist systemic evils such as imperial domination, the maintenance of nuclear weapons, and the death penalty. Unfortunately, states Dear, most U.S. Christians are good-hearted people who support war and violence because they have been duped by misguided leaders and institutions. Dear is interviewed by Stephen Morris, a theology student at Regis College in Toronto, Canada.

As you read, consider the following questions:

1. Why does Dear avoid the use of the word *pacifist*?
2. According to Dear, how can Christians learn to "let God disarm our hearts"?
3. Where should the church focus its energy, in Dear's view?

John Dear and Stephen Morris, "Non-Violence or Non-Existence: An Interview with John Dear, S.J.," *Catholic New Times*, vol. 27, December 14, 2003, pp. 14–15. Copyright © 2003 by Catholic New Times, Inc. Reproduced by permission.

*S*tephen Morris: *How do you think the early Christians would have reacted to something like a draft currently promoted by the Bush administration?*

John Dear: First of all, this is to be expected. The U.S. is a blatant empire, dominating the world shamelessly, with total disregard for human life, and we're seeing that played out in Iraq. Unfortunately most people are just going right along with it, including most Christians in the U.S. But as I understand it, that's not the way it was a long, long time ago. For the first 300 years of Christianity, being a Christian meant you were not going to worship the Emperor, you were not going to join the imperial army, you refused to kill, you said that you were worshipping this guy Jesus. They immediately arrested you and they fed you to the lions. So all the early Christians were people of nonviolence, and some were martyred.

Then in 315 Constantine converted and soon after that the Just War theory began and here we are 1700 years later with Christians rejecting the Sermon on the Mount, and picking up arms.

The Non-Violence of Jesus

Why do Jesus, the early Christians and pacifists say, "It is unlawful for me to fight?"

For one thing, I don't really use that word "pacifist." It sounds too much like the word "passive." I like that clumsy word of Gandhi and Martin Luther King, "non-violence," because in it is the phrase, "You will do no violence to anyone." But the whole point of Christianity as I understand it is that we are following Jesus and the only thing that you can say about Jesus for sure is that he was non-violent. He said we have to love one another, serve one another, be compassionate with one another, and then this—we must love our enemies. You cannot love your enemies and bomb them at the same time, or plan to kill them, or maintain 30,000 nuclear weapons to destroy the planet. Then you are no longer following Jesus. Gandhi said that Jesus was the most active practitioner of nonviolence in the history of the world and the only people who don't know that Jesus was non-violent are Christians.

You cannot support war, no matter what your government

tells you, because you are following Jesus. And his last words to the community as they were dragging him away after they arrested him were: "Put down the sword!" We're not allowed to take up the sword or drop a bomb or threaten others with nuclear weapons.

Disarming One's Heart

You talk about "disarming one's heart." Can you explain what you mean by that?

I've been studying Gandhi and King and Dorothy Day for all these years and I think that non-violence is not just a strategy or a tactic but a way of living. And it begins in the heart with a vision of a reconciled humanity, a vision that every human being is a sister or brother, that we are all children of the God of peace. We're already reconciled, already one, already united—and if you really believe that, if you enter into the spiritual vision of reality, you can never hurt or never kill another human being ever again, much less remain silent while war is waged or starvation exists and nuclear weapons are maintained. So non-violence is this active way of love and truth that seeks justice and peace for the whole world, seeking reconciliation with everyone, deliberately resisting this systemic evil, and it operates on this one condition: there is no cause by which we would support the taking of a single human life.

I'm willing to accept suffering to undergo violence without a trace of retaliation. I'm willing to be killed, but I'm never ready to kill, as I pursue this vision of a unified human family. So non-violence is a whole way of life. Gandhi said it's a life-force more powerful than all the weapons of the world combined and we're just beginning to tap into it. But it begins in our heart that often. We're so used to violence, that's all we know.

I've come to the conclusion that we're all so violent that the only way to do the hard part really is with prayer and meditation, and I see this in everyone from St. Francis to Gandhi. You have to turn to the God of peace, and let God disarm our hearts so that we can become disarming people. It's a contemplative thing, a life of prayer, but it's also an active life. You have to be part of the movement.

Christianity and Nonviolence

I never really wanted to be a pacifist. I first believed [theologian] Reinhold Niebuhr when he insisted that if you desire justice, you had better be ready to kill someone along the way. But John Howard Yoder, in his extraordinary book *The Politics of Jesus*, convinced me that at the heart of the Christian faith is the conviction that Christ chose to die on the cross rather than achieve the world's redemption through violence. The defeat of death through resurrection makes it both possible and necessary that Christians live nonviolently in a world of violence. . . .

Christian nonviolence is no less than the very form and character of life to which we are called by Christ. It is but another name for the friendship we believe God has made possible, a friendship that constitutes the alternative to the violence that grips our lives and our world.

Stanley Hauerwas, *Other Side*, November/December 2002.

The False Spirituality of Violence

Some say the world is post-Christian. Some lament this but do you think the church might return to a more prophetic stance regarding war, given that Pope John Paul II totally condemned the invasion of Iraq. Are you hopeful?

A: I want it to go in that direction. I thought the whole point of the church was to follow the non-violent Jesus, which means the church is supposed to be a community of active nonviolence. The church can never support war or hold up some baloney called the Just War doctrine. It has nothing to do with Jesus. We've just gotten totally co-opted; we're part of the power structure by and large, to the point that the night before the bombing of Iraq, [TV evangelist] Billy Graham prayed with [George W.] Bush in the White House and the prayer went something to the effect of: "May the bombs hit the targets and kill the enemy, in the name of our Lord Jesus." And nobody is fazed by that! They've totally missed the point of the Gospel, and are into idolatry, and blasphemy, and heresy, and this false spirituality of violence that justifies empire.

The church needs to disentangle from power and stay at the bottom with the poor, the victims and the marginalized; then it will move closer towards Jesus and the gospel. And the more it rejects war and renounces the Just War theory, the more it will turn to the Sermon on the Mount and its commandment to love our enemies, and once we start doing that, we will become prophetic people and say that war is never blessed by God and you cannot follow Jesus by supporting war no matter what the president wants to tell us.

Here in the U.S. people are numb, very comfortable and most of them are waving the flag and going to church, being very proud about the U.S. and the war in Iraq and totally oblivious to our huge arsenal of weapons of mass destruction. In effect, we are placing our security in our government and weapons and not in God.

People Are Too Comfortable

A reviewer of [documentary filmmaker] Michael Moore's book said that his position was basically that Americans are kindhearted people who have been duped by an evil system. What if this is not the case? What if Americans are perfectly aware of their power and position in the world, and want to take full advantage of it? How would you respond to this?

A: It might be true. As I travel around the country I meet people who are by and large very good people, but gosh, we're just so comfortable that we're just clueless. I saw widespread support for the war, even among the churches, and I see wide support for our nuclear weapons and the death penalty, and anti-immigration policies, racism, and violence in general. But however we describe the situation, we're a very sick people. The phrase I use is "addicted to violence." We're so addicted we don't even know what we're doing. My hope is in the great examples of King and Dorothy Day, and the non-violence now being discussed in the churches. I also take consolation that the peace movement in the Christian community is just beginning. We are just learning what non-violence requires, just starting to organize for a new world without war.

*"The apostle Paul specifically teaches that
God instituted governments to practice
violence in certain instances."*

Christians Should Not Reject the Just Use of Violence

Mark Galli

Christians need not reject the use of violence in all situations, argues Mark Galli in the following viewpoint. Sometimes it is necessary to use violence to defend oneself and others from unjust attacks, he contends. In the Bible, moreover, neither Jesus nor the apostles required soldiers to give up their arms in order to become Christians. While Christians should avoid personal retaliation or the use of violence to promote their faith, they should also accept the necessary use of violence in government-directed military combat, Galli maintains. Galli is managing editor of *Christianity Today*, a monthly magazine of evangelical Christian opinion.

As you read, consider the following questions:

1. According to Galli, what specific stories in the Bible reveal that soldiers can become Christians without abandoning their duties?
2. According to John Calvin, quoted by the author, how does a magistrate dishonor God?
3. Who were some of the soldier-martyrs in the Roman army during the early Christian era, according to Galli?

S hortly after the terrorist attack on September 11 [2001], the Dorothy Day Catholic Worker House in Washington, D.C., proclaimed, "If we kill as a response to this great tragedy, we are no better than the terrorists who launched this awful offensive. Killing is killing, and killing is wrong."

Not only pacifists but also moderates seem to share this basic view. Theologian Miroslov Volf, while acknowledging the justness of a military response to the attack on the U.S., also said, "Taking a life is always the wrong thing."

Yet few people are aware of what a stunningly new thing this is—for Christians of all stripes and backgrounds to eschew all violence. Disillusionment with the military after Vietnam surely contributed to it, as has a growing repugnance for suffering, blood, and death in our antiseptic culture. But two historical assumptions seem to drive many believers' thinking on this matter.

Biblical Soldiers

The first assumption is that the New Testament is uniformly against violence. In *The Moral Vision of the New Testament*, pacifist Richard Hays utters something many nonpacifists affirm: "From Matthew to Revelation, we find a consistent witness against violence and a calling to the community to follow the example of Jesus in accepting suffering rather than inflicting it."

It's a sweeping sentiment that, it turns out, sweeps too broadly. When John the Baptist told soldiers to repent, he did not ask them to forsake their professions. He simply told them to soldier with integrity. When Jesus meets a Roman centurion, far from commanding him to give up his calling, he praises the man for his great faith. When Roman commander Cornelius becomes a Christian, he is not told in his dreams or by the apostles that laying down his arms is a necessary condition of faith in Christ. And Paul speaks of believers in the Praetorian Guard—men trained to defend the emperor by force when called upon.

More directly, the apostle Paul specifically teaches that God instituted governments to practice violence in certain instances. John Calvin later intensified the point to bring out its deeper meaning: A magistrate dishonors God if he refuses to "bloody his sword" in pursuing justice and defending people from evildoers.

Nonviolent Tactics Do Not Always Work

We often find ourselves having to decide to use violence and military might in order to resist a greater evil. Sometimes, the tactics of nonviolence will not work. Gandhi's tactics worked against the British, because the British had a basic sense of morality and justice, and were capable of recognizing their own injustice when nonviolence made it clear to them. Dr. [Martin Luther] King's tactics worked because Caucasian Americans had a basic sense of morality and justice and were able to recognize our own injustice when nonviolence made it clear. It is difficult to imagine that such tactics would have worked against the Third Reich, who gassed six million people and burnt their bodies without recognizing any injustice. It is difficult to imagine nonviolent tactics working against [the terrorist group] Al Qaida who could crash loaded airliners into occupied office buildings and not recognize their own injustice.

Sometimes nonviolent tactics are not likely to work and we must face the prospects that if we act with military might, some might die. But if we don't act, more will die.

Kenneth G. Page, church sermon, September 1, 2002.

To be sure, the New Testament uniformly teaches that we are never to use violence to promote or defend our faith (and the world would be a much safer place right now if every religion and sect would adopt this principle). On the other hand, the New Testament, from Matthew to Revelation, seems to accept the fact that some Christians will practice violence as members of the military.

On Rendering to Caesar

The second historical assumption is that the early church stood uniformly against all violence. The early church Fathers certainly taught Christians to refuse to retaliate when persecuted—this refusal became a Christian distinction, in fact. And Hippolytus, third-century bishop of Rome, announced that he wouldn't baptize any who refused to give up soldiering.

But often it is not clear whether the problem is violence or idolatry. Every soldier was supposedly asked to offer incense to Caesar—though the requirement was often neglected for long periods. This would explain why by 303, ten years before Constantine became a Christian (a decade before the early church supposedly compromised its ethics as it came into power), the Roman army was littered with Christians. That year Diocletian began ferreting out Christians in his army, which turned out to be a simple matter: they were the only ones who refused to sacrifice to the genius of Caesar.

As a result, we now have hundreds of soldier-martyr stories from that era, like that of Sebastian of Gaul [Narbonne], captain of the Praetorian Guard, and George of Beirut, a high-ranking officer of noble birth. But apart from the demands of politico-religious emperor worship, many Christians were able to function as leaders in the Roman army.

This is not the place to argue the fine points of ethics and history. Suffice it to say that early Christians did not conclude that "all killing is wrong" or assume that Jesus' teaching regarding personal retaliation applied directly to larger political arrangements. In short, they seemed to have had a more nuanced view of violence than we seem capable of in our day.

| "*We have become a nation of religious adherents in self-imposed straightjackets, indifferent to much of the suffering and injustice in our midst.*"

Activism Is the Best Way to Achieve Social Justice

George J. Bryjak

Although America has the highest degree of religiosity of any of the world's modern industrial nations, most religious Americans do not act on their beliefs when confronted with social injustice, writes George J. Bryjak in the following viewpoint. The nation's high levels of inequality prove that there is a gap between religious belief and social concern. This gap reveals the influence of social Darwinism—the notion that the privileged are evolutionarily superior and deserving of prosperity—in U.S. culture, Bryjak explains. While a few religious leaders, such as Martin Luther King Jr., have rightly applied their beliefs in the struggle for social justice, most Americans see spirituality as a journey of personal salvation that has no connection to social activism and institutional change. Bryjak is a sociology professor at the University of San Diego.

As you read, consider the following questions:

1. According to the Pew Research Center survey cited by the author, what percentage of Americans claims that "religion plays an important role in their lives"?
2. Who was Herbert Spencer, according to Bryjak?
3. In what way has religion become a commodity in the United States, in Bryjak's opinion?

George J. Bryjak, "U.S. Religiosity in a Self-Imposed Straightjacket," *National Catholic Reporter*, vol. 39, March 28, 2003, pp. 22–23. Copyright © 2003 by *National Catholic Reporter*, www.natcath.org. Reproduced by permission.

A recent international survey conducted by the Pew Research Center found six in 10 Americans agreeing that "religion plays an important role in their lives," by far the highest of any modern industrial society investigated. This figure represents approximately twice as many self-proclaimed religious adherents as reside in Great Britain, Italy and Canada, and about five times more than in France, the Czech Republic and Japan.

Rampant Inequality

The paradox of the Pew findings in the wealthy nations surveyed is that high religious affiliation is associated with low levels of equality across societal institutions and policies and vice versa. For example, a 2001 World Health Organization report of 191 countries found that the United States ranked 37th in overall health care services behind almost every European country as well as Morocco, Oman and Costa Rica. A just-released study by the Robert Wood Johnson Foundation concluded that nearly one in three non-elderly Americans (about 75 million people) did not have medical coverage for some period over the past two years. While many believers in this country are apparently content with a medical system that excludes millions of their fellows, individuals in significantly less religious France and Italy have created health care systems ranked one and two in the world respectively.

We have the highest degree of economic inequality in the industrialized world. The Washington-based Economic Policy Institute notes that while the wealthiest 1 percent of stockholders account for just under 50 percent of all stocks by value, one of every six children lives below the official poverty line.

Full-time working women earn about 77 percent of what full-time employed men do in the United States. In Great Britain, Italy and France, these figures are 80, 82 and 88 percent respectively. Among modern industrial states, Japan alone lags substantially behind the United States in economic gender equity.

Only the United States continues to execute offenders—including, on occasion, mentally retarded individuals—despite recent findings that the criminal justice system is replete with errors, and that the capital punishment convictions of factually innocent defendants are hardly uncommon.

Veley. © by Bradford Veley. Reproduced by permission.

At a time when most prosperous nations have a system of compulsory military service, the United States maintains voluntary armed forces. Fighting and dying on the battlefield have become the plight of lower- and middle-class males, while sons of the wealthy stay home and enjoy the economic benefits of their privileged positions.

Do unto Others?

What is it about our religious beliefs or the relation between religion and other institutions that has prevented the weaving of the golden rule into the fabric of American society as it has in more secular nations? In other words, why do the religious convictions of so many Americans exist in a kind of schizophrenic detachment from their brethren in the wider social world?

To begin, we seem to be of two minds when it comes to social justice issues and the application of the "do unto others" dictum. As far as helping victims of tragedies such as the recent terrorist attacks and natural disasters, we Americans have always been generous with our time and money. However, as a nation we are unwilling to institutionalize our individual good will on issues such as universal health coverage, a livable minimum wage, and gender and racial equality. We are loath to help people designated as unworthy of societal generosity, as in the distinction between the "deserving" and the "undeserving" poor.

A partial explanation for the gap between religious beliefs and societal practice can be found in the nation's intellectual history. English philosopher and pioneering sociologist Herbert Spencer (1820–1903), whose Social Darwinism swept across the United States in the 1880s (the term "survival of the fittest" comes from Spencer, not Charles Darwin), gave a pronounced boost to a mindset of rugged individualism already entrenched in this country.

According to Spencer, wherever one found himself or herself in the system of inequality that's where he or she deserved to be. Wealth was a natural outgrowth of intellectual and moral superiority, while poverty was a product of intellectual and moral inferiority. By definition, the wealthy were justly prosperous, the poor rightly impoverished. Yale professor William Graham Sumner (Spencer's most prominent American disciple) wrote a 145-page treatise titled "What Social Classes Owe Each Other" that can be summarized in a single harsh phrase: nothing at all.

Religion as Commodity

For all of our self-proclaimed piety and impressive rates of church attendance, it appears that the golden rule has been overwhelmed by Spencer's legacy and smothered by the thick veneer of narcissistic materialism that is contemporary American culture. We strive to be the richest ("fittest") in a culture where, as sociologist Richard Robbins notes, "virtually all of our everyday activities—work, leisure, the fulfillment of social responsibilities—take place in the context of commodities."

Complete with rock bands and laser light shows, some forms of religious expression are more entertainment than devotion as spirituality is reduced to another commodity to be bought and sold in the marketplace. My guess is that for many of these adherents, *Jesus Christ Superstar* has the same impact on their lives as Mariah Carey superstar.

Finally, over the past 40 years there has been a shift in religious orientation on the part of many, emphasizing a "one-to-one" relation with God and redemption as a personal journey. This spiritual orientation separates people from concerns about, and participation in, the larger society. With the rise of "God Box" or television preachers, one need not leave the house to experience religious fulfillment.

To be sure, not all religious adherents and leaders have succumbed to lives wherein success is measured by material possessions and salvation is a solitary journey. The relentless struggle of Martin Luther King Jr. and others illustrates how people have made enormous sacrifices working collectively for social and economic justice. Unfortunately, these individuals are a minority of the population. The true religion of contemporary American society is consumption, as an excursion to our real houses of worship—shopping malls—will attest.

Indifferent to Suffering

The United States appears to be the lone wealthy nation where an undercurrent of Social Darwinism intersects with crass materialism and an exclusionary, personal quest for salvation to yield a narrow interpretation of the golden rule. This is a rendition wherein individuals comfort family and friends but refrain from striving for equality and justice at the societal level.

A man of deep religious convictions, the 19th-century Danish philosopher Soren Kierkegaard had nothing but disdain for what he called "Christendom," the "herd" mentality of worshipers who weekly marched into churches as if attending a social function, then stomped out again, indifferent to the true message of their faith. For Kierkegaard, "Being a Christian in Christendom . . . is as impossible as doing gymnastics in a straightjacket." We have become a nation of religious adherents in self-imposed straightjackets, indifferent to much of the suffering and injustice in our midst.

| *"If you want justice, a great place to start is by working for morality."*

Emphasizing Personal Morality Is the Best Way to Achieve Social Justice

Doug Tattershall

In the following viewpoint Doug Tattershall decries the fact that religious people who emphasize personal morality are often denigrated as fundamentalists while those who promote social justice are depicted as a struggling benevolent minority. In the Catholic Church, for example, social justice advocates receive praise in the media even though they support such non-Catholic goals as legal abortion and homosexual marriage. In Tattershall's opinion the "social justice Catholics" actually contribute to social problems by neglecting personal morality. He concludes that the best way for religious people to work for social justice is by emphasizing personal morality. Tattershall is the media relations coordinator for the Lexington Public Library in Lexington, Kentucky.

As you read, consider the following questions:

1. How has social justice come to be defined, in Tattershall's opinion?
2. According to the author, why do "personal morality Catholics" feel guilty about not emphasizing social justice enough?
3. What has aggravated the problems of poverty, illegitimacy, and overcrowded prisons, in Tattershall's view?

Doug Tattershall, "If You Want Justice, Work for Morality," *New Oxford Review*, vol. LXIX, October 2002, pp. 43–44. Copyright © 2002 by *New Oxford Review*. Reproduced by permission.

I heard it from the pulpit one day at Mass, so it must be true. The division in the Catholic Church isn't a matter of dissent versus fidelity. It's not even a matter of liberal versus conservative. It's a matter of those who emphasize social justice versus those who emphasize personal morality, and we really need both to be fully Catholic. So let us stand and profess our faith. . . .

Wait a second, Padre.

I know a lot of "personal morality Catholics" who think oppressing the poor and defrauding laborers of their wages are sins that cry to Heaven for vengeance. However, I see a lot of "social justice Catholics" advocating a justice that includes handing out condoms, legal abortion, easy divorce, and homosexual "marriage." So much for the two sides complementing each other.

Social Justice vs. Personal Morality

This "social justice vs. personal morality" divide has the convenience of presenting both sides as legitimately Catholic— they both are faithful, they just emphasize different aspects of the faith, right? It's a pleasant thought, the idea that our division really isn't a division, and if by social justice Catholics we mean the Missionaries of Charity, it would be true. But nowadays so-called social justice Catholics tend to be rather ambivalent about the Missionaries of Charity and others like them. They'll give the good nuns a pat on the head for their nice work with the poorest of the poor, but it really isn't social justice in their book. Mother Teresa's missionaries aren't nearly political enough and they're far too faithful to the Church's idea of personal morality.

That's because social justice, as it has come to be understood, isn't about service and charity so much as it is about advocacy. And not just advocacy, but advocacy with a particular—i.e., secular liberal—slant. Service and charity tend to get left to the Pollyannas of the world, the same Pollyannas who think that abortion is murder and that a boy and a girl shouldn't have sex until they get married.

It isn't easy being a Pollyanna. You say your beads, confess your sins, maybe pick up donated baby supplies for unwed mothers or deliver food vouchers to poor families. And for all your effort, if you're noticed at all, you have the privilege of being labeled "fundamentalist" or "religious Right"—America's equivalent to the Taliban.

Spiritual and Moral Renewal

Real moral sentiments are not yet fully gone in the general population, and they can be invigorated once again. Clearly, for Christians such as the present writer, a real renewal calls for repentance, conversion, and new determination to follow Christ, "the author and finisher of faith" (Hebrews 12:2). Short of a spiritual renewal, moral improvement is by no means impossible, although from the Christian perspective it is more difficult, because it must be achieved by one's own strength and efforts alone. It will certainly be facilitated in the general society when men and women of faith begin to think and live consistently with the principles that they officially espouse and thus set good examples for others.

Religion & Society Report, October 2003.

Meanwhile, social justice Catholics wring their hands, raise awareness, feel your pain (if you're lucky enough to be born), and in their more introspective moments, light candles. For their effort, they are oft-sought and oft-quoted by reporters national and local as those few good people in that big bad Church. Especially if they're willing to trash the big bad Church's teachings on personal morality.

Some Disturbing Facts

Since personal morality Catholics believe oppression and persecution are sins, they're likely to feel guilty about the idea that they don't emphasize social justice enough—personal morality Catholics are great at guilt, because there's always more work we could be doing. But before you line up at the confessional (if your parish is fortunate enough to have a line at the confessional) and before you start wondering if maybe you should stop being so "rigid" about personal morality for the sake of social justice, remember this:

• *One of the strongest indicators of child poverty is the number of parents in a home.* Single-parent families struggle. More than 40 percent of children in female-headed families are poor, according to the most recent *Kids Count Data Book* by

The Annie E. Casey Foundation. But what are social justice Catholics doing to defend chastity and marriage?

• *Single-parent homes increase as availability of contraception increases.* Pope Paul VI predicted in *Humanae Vitae* in 1968 that increased use of contraception would lead to marital infidelity and lower moral standards. Since then, divorce and illegitimate births have indeed increased, thus aggravating the problem of child poverty. But what are social justice Catholics doing to defend *Humanae Vitae*?

• *Prison populations are disproportionately made up of men from broken homes.* Boys raised without their biological fathers in the home are twice as likely to end up in prison than boys from intact families, according to a study by Ivy League scholars presented to the American Sociological Association. But what are social justice Catholics doing to defend fatherhood?

Morality Leads to Justice

The fact is, personal morality is critical to social justice, and advocates for such things as free sex, free contraceptives, and no-fault divorce have only aggravated the problems of child poverty, illegitimate births, and overcrowded prisons. The social justice Catholics who neglect personal morality are part of the problem. They aren't half-right, because they aren't even getting the half they emphasize right.

If you want justice, a great place to start is by working for morality.

Periodical Bibliography

The following articles have been selected to supplement the diverse views presented in this chapter.

Dave Andrusko	"'Holy Abortion' and the Religious Coalition for Reproductive Choice," *National Right to Life News*, May 2003.
John W. Bowling	"Violent Temptations," *Christian Social Action*, May/June 2003.
Allan Brill	"Liberals Get Cross-Wise: The Christian Left Is the Progressive Stool's Third Leg," *Progressive Populist*, May 15, 2004.
John Bryson Chane	"Fighting Fundamentalism with Fundamentalism Won't Bring Peace," *Witness*, March/April 2003.
Dolores Curran	"There Is a Lot to Be Said for Less," *U.S. Catholic*, February 1999.
Stanley Hauerwas	"Nonviolence and the War Without End: The Current War Challenges Christians to Grasp More Deeply than Ever the Nonviolence at the Heart of Our Identity and Our Vocation," *Other Side*, November/December 2002.
Stanley Kurtz	"Beyond Gay Marriage," *Weekly Standard*, August 11, 2003.
Elizabeth Lesser	"Twenty-first-Century Spirituality," *Tikkun*, January/February 2000.
Peter C. Meilaender	"Christians as Patriots," *First Things*, February 2003.
Eugene F. Rogers Jr.	"Sanctified Unions: An Argument for Gay Marriage," *Christian Century*, June 15, 2004.
Melissa Snarr	"The University of Social Justice: Beyond Community Service, Colleges Educate for Social Change," *Sojourners*, May/June 2003.
David C. Stolinsky	"Our Titanic Nonjudgmentalism," *New Oxford Review*, April 2000.
John M. Swomley	"Abortion as a Positive Moral Choice," *Human Quest*, July/August 1999.
Jim Wallis	"Gays and Marriage: A Middle Way," *Catholic New Times*, December 14, 2003.
Benjamin D. Wiker	"The Death of Morality," *Crisis*, July/August 2004.

For Further Discussion

Chapter 1

1. Jeff Jacoby maintains that religious belief was essential to the founding of America, while Robin Morgan contends that the founders generally embraced secularism and rejected the mixing of religion with politics. What evidence does each author include to support his or her argument? Whose evidence do you find to be more persuasive? Why?

2. Samuel Huntington argues that America is a religious nation strongly committed to its Christian identity. Jesse Walker argues that a growing number of people are challenging the traditions of their own religion or are fusing elements of other faiths into their own. Do you find one author's viewpoint to be more convincing than the other? Or do you agree with both authors? Why? Cite the viewpoints as you defend your answer.

3. Both the Center on Religion and Society and Edward Tabash provide examples of discrimination or prejudice in support of their views. Can you think of examples of discrimination from your own experience or those of people you know that coincide with the arguments of either of these authors? Please describe them.

Chapter 2

1. The viewpoints of both Leith Anderson and Frank R. Zindler were written for very specific audiences. Anderson was writing for evangelical Christians, while Zindler was speaking to a gathering of atheists. Reexamine their viewpoints and select the supporting arguments that you think would find greater acceptance among a more mixed or general audience. Then select the arguments that would not likely be embraced by such an audience. Explain the reasoning behind your grouping of the arguments.

2. The editors of *Report Newsmagazine* contend that the term "fundamentalist" is often wrongly equated with "extremist" and "terrorist." How does Karen Armstrong define fundamentalism? Which of these authors' definitions of fundamentalism is more accurate, in your opinion? Explain.

3. After reading the viewpoints by Ronnie Dugger and *Christianity Today*, are you more or less likely to feel concerned when you hear a politician express religious convictions? Explain your answer.

Chapter 3

1. After reading the first two viewpoints in this chapter, do you believe that the inclusion of the phrase "under God" in the Pledge

of Allegiance violates the First Amendment's clause prohibiting a governmental establishment of religion? Why or why not?

2. Krista Kafer maintains that "schools can create numerous opportunities for [religious] learning and expression in public schools." Do you agree that it is appropriate for schools to provide opportunities for student-led religious expression in public schools? Or do you think that such provisions constitute a breach of church-state separation? Explain.

3. Avi Schick supports the proposed Workplace Religious Freedom Act (WRFA), which would provide stronger protections for the rights of religious employees. Why does the American Civil Liberties Union oppose the 2004 version of the WRFA? Do you think that Schick would agree with the concerns voiced by the ACLU? Use citations from the viewpoints as you explain your answer.

Chapter 4

1. Both Amy Hetrick and Concerned Women for America cite the personal experiences of others to buttress their respective arguments for and against religious support of abortion rights. In your opinion, which author uses these personal anecdotes to better effect? Why?

2. The Religious Institute on Sexual Morality, Justice, and Healing maintains that there are scripturally based arguments for same-sex marriage. Does the viewpoint by David Neff effectively refute this contention of the Religious Institute? Why or why not?

3. Mark Galli maintains that early Christians "had a more nuanced view of violence than we seem capable of in our day." Do you think that John Dear's peace activism and promotion of nonviolence reveals a lack of nuance and complexity in his thinking? Defend your answer with evidence from the viewpoints.

4. George J. Bryjak argues that religious Americans tend to neglect social justice issues. Doug Tattershall maintains that social justice advocates typically neglect morality issues. How do the arguments of these two authors reflect differing definitions of social justice and morality? Explain.

Organizations to Contact

The editors have compiled the following list of organizations concerned with the issues debated in this book. The descriptions are derived from materials provided by the organizations. All have publications or information available for interested readers. The list was compiled on the date of publication of the present volume; the information provided here may change. Be aware that many organizations take several weeks or longer to respond to inquiries, so allow as much time as possible.

American Atheists
PO Box 5733, Parsippany, NJ 07054-6733
(908) 276-7300 • (908) 276-7402
e-mail: info@atheists.org • Web site: www.atheists.org

American Atheists is an educational organization dedicated to the complete and absolute separation of church and state. It opposes religious involvement such as prayer and religious clubs in public schools. The organization's purpose is to stimulate freedom of thought and inquiry concerning religious beliefs and practices. It publishes the monthly journal *American Atheist*.

American Center for Law and Justice (ACLJ)
PO Box 64429, Virginia Beach, VA 23467
(757) 226-2489 • fax: (757) 226-2836
e-mail: aclj@exis.net • Web site: www.aclj.org

The center is a public interest law firm and educational organization dedicated to promoting life, liberty, and the family. ACLJ provides legal services and support to attorneys and others who are involved in defending the religious and civil liberties of Americans. It publishes the booklets *Students' Rights and the Public Schools* and *Christian Rights in the Workplace*.

American Civil Liberties Union (ACLU)
125 Broad St., 18th Fl., New York, NY 10004
(212) 549-2585
Web site: www.aclu.org

The ACLU is a national organization that works to defend Americans' civil rights guaranteed in the U.S. Constitution, including rights of religious expression. It opposes excessive entanglement of church and state. Its publications include the handbook *The Right to Religious Liberty* and the semiannual newsletter *Civil Liberties Alert*.

Americans United for Separation of Church and State (AU)
518 C St. NE, Washington, DC 20002
(202) 466-3234 • fax: (202) 466-2587
e-mail: americansunited@au.org • Web site: www.au.org
AU works to protect the constitutional principle of church-state separation. It opposes mandatory prayer in public schools, tax dollars for parochial schools, and religious groups' participating in politics. AU publishes the monthly *Church & State* magazine as well as issue papers, legislative alerts, reference materials, and books.

Center for Progressive Christianity
99 Brattle St., Cambridge, MA 02138
(617) 441-0928 • fax: (617) 441-6201
e-mail: office@tcpc.org • Web site: www.tcpc.org
The Center for Progressive Christianity provides various networking opportunities and resources for progressive churches, organizations, individuals, and others with connections to Christianity. The center promotes the use of sound scholarship, free inquiry, and a respect for religious diversity. Its Web site includes an online library of articles and reviews as well as links to material published on other sites.

Christian Coalition of America
PO Box 37030, Washington, DC 20013-7030
(202) 479-6900 • fax: (202) 479-4260
e-mail: coalition@cc.org • Web site: www.cc.org
Founded by evangelist Pat Robertson, the coalition is a grassroots political organization working to provide voter education and to stop what it believes is the moral decay of government. Its Web site includes links to news articles, action alerts, and current advocacy and legislative campaigns of concern to evangelical and conservative Christians.

Concerned Women for America (CWA)
1015 Fifteenth St. NW, Suite 1100, Washington, DC 20005
(202) 488-7000 • fax: (202) 488-0806
e-mail: mail@cwfa.org • Web site: www.cwfa.org
CWA works to strengthen marriage and the traditional family according to Judeo-Christian moral standards. It opposes abortion, pornography, feminism, and homosexuality. The organization publishes numerous brochures and policy papers as well as *Family Voice*, a monthly newsmagazine.

Council for Secular Humanism
PO Box 664, Amherst, NY 14226-0664
(716) 636-7571 • fax: (716) 636-1733
e-mail: info@secularhumanism.org
Web site: www.secularhumanism.org

The council is an educational organization dedicated to fostering the growth of democracy, secular humanism, and the principles of free inquiry. It publishes the quarterly magazine *Free Inquiry*, and its Web site includes an online library containing such articles as "Why the Christian Right Is Wrong About Homosexuality" and "Responding to the Religious Right."

Eagle Forum
PO Box 618, Alton, IL 62002
(618) 462-5415 • fax: (618) 462-8909
e-mail: eagle@eagleforum.org • Web site: www.eagleforum.org

Eagle Forum is a Christian group that promotes morality and traditional family values as revealed through a conservative interpretation of the Bible. It opposes many facets of public education and liberal government. The forum publishes the monthly *Phyllis Schlafly Report* and a periodic newsletter.

FaithfulAmerica.org
e-mail: info@faithfulamerica.org
Web site: www.faithfulamerica.org

A project of the National Council of Churches, FaithfulAmerica.org is an online community of people of faith working to build a more just and compassionate nation. It aspires to be an online wing of a new progressive religious movement, similar to the ones that fought for independence, abolition, and civil rights. Its Web site includes links to complementary organizations and offers one-click opportunities to write elected officials, sign petitions, donate to causes, and contact the media.

Family Research Council
801 G St. NW, Washington, DC 20001
(202) 393-2100 • fax: (800) 225-4008
Web site: www.frc.org

The council is a research, resource, and educational organization that promotes the traditional family, which it defines as a group of people bound by marriage, blood, or adoption. The council publishes numerous periodicals from a conservative perspective, including *Culture Facts*, a weekly report, and *Washington Watch*, a monthly newsletter. Its Web site contains an online archive of papers and publications on religion and public life, arts and culture, education, and other issues.

Freedom from Religion Foundation, Inc.

PO Box 750, Madison, WI 53701
(608) 256-8900
e-mail: ffrf@mailbag.com • Web site: www.ffrf.org

The foundation works to keep state and church separate and to educate the public about the views of freethinkers, agnostics, and nontheists. Its publications include the newspaper *Freethought Today* and the books *Losing Faith in Faith: From Preacher to Atheist* and *The Born Again Skeptic's Guide to the Bible.*

Heritage Foundation

214 Massachusetts Ave. NE, Washington, DC 20002-4999
(202) 546-4400 • fax: (202) 546-8328
e-mail: info@heritage.org • Web site: www.heritage.org

The foundation is a conservative public policy research institute that advocates traditional American values, free-market economics, and limited government. It occasionally publishes articles on religion in American life in its publications, which include the monthly *Policy Review.*

Interfaith Alliance

1331 H St. NW, 11th Fl., Washington, DC 20005
(202) 639-6370 • fax: (202) 639-6375
e-mail: tia@interfaithalliance.org
Web site: www.interfaithalliance.org

The interfaith alliance is a nonpartisan, clergy-led grassroots organization that advances a mainstream, faith-based political agenda. Its membership, which draws from more than fifty faith traditions, promotes religion as a healing and constructive force in public life. It publishes the *Light*, a quarterly newsletter.

People for the American Way Foundation

2000 M St. NW, Suite 400, Washington, DC 20036
(202) 467-4999 • fax: (800) 326-7329
e-mail: pfaw@pfaw.org • Web site: www.pfaw.org

People for the American Way Foundation is a nonprofit, nonpartisan organization that works to increase tolerance and respect for America's diverse cultures, religions, and values such as freedom of expression. The foundation's Web site includes Right Wing Watch, an online library of information about right-wing organizations, and the Progressive Network, a database with links to progressive organizations across the country.

Pluralism Project

Harvard University
201 Vanserg Hall, 25 Francis Ave., Cambridge, MA 02138
(617) 496-2481 • fax: (617) 496-2428
e-mail: staff@pluralism.org • Web site: www.pluralism.org

The Pluralism Project was founded by Harvard University professor Diana L. Eck to study and document the growing religious diversity in the United States, with a special focus on immigrant religious communities. It publishes the CD-ROM *On Common Ground: World Religions in America* and furnishes articles and other information on its Web site.

Toward Tradition

PO Box 58, Mercer Island, WA 98040
(206) 236-3046 • fax: (206) 236-3288
Web site: www.towardtradition.org

Toward Tradition is a national educational movement of Jews and Christians and other Americans seeking to advance the nation toward traditional, faith-based, American principles of constitutional and limited government, the rule of law, representative democracy, free markets, a strong military, and a moral public culture. It disseminates position papers from its Web site and distributes a newsletter.

Bibliography of Books

Sydney E. Ahlstrom   *A Religious History of the American People.* New Haven, CT: Yale University Press, 2004.

Kimberly Baker, ed.   *The Fundamentals of Extremism: The Christian Right in America.* New Boston, MI: New Boston Books, 2003.

William J. Bennett   *The Broken Hearth: Reversing the Moral Collapse of the American Family.* New York: Doubleday, 2001.

Stephen L. Carter   *God's Name in Vain: The Wrongs and Rights of Religion in Politics.* New York: Basic Books, 2000.

Mark Chaves   *Congregations in America.* Cambridge, MA: Harvard University Press, 2004.

Joan Chittister   *In Search of Belief.* Liguori, MO: Liguori/Triumph, 1999.

John Dear   *Living Peace: A Spirituality of Contemplation and Action.* New York: Doubleday, 2001.

Daniel L. Dreisbach   *Thomas Jefferson and the Wall of Separation Between Church and State.* New York: New York University Press, 2002.

Bruce David Forbes and Jeffrey H. Mahan, eds.   *Religion and Popular Culture in America.* Berkeley and Los Angeles: University of California Press, 2000.

Samuel P. Huntington   *Who Are We? The Challenges to America's Identity.* New York: Simon & Schuster, 2004.

William R. Hutchison   *Religious Pluralism in America: The Contentious History of a Founding Ideal.* New Haven, CT: Yale University Press, 2003.

Michael Kelly and Lynn M. Messina, eds.   *Religion in Politics and Society.* New York: H.W. Wilson, 2002.

Paul Kreeft   *How to Win the Culture War: A Christian Battle Plan for a Society in Crisis.* Downers Grove, IL: InterVarsity, 2002.

Peter Augustine Lawler   *Aliens in America: The Strange Truth About Our Souls.* Wilmington, DE: ISI Books, 2002.

Michael Lerner   *Spirit Matters.* Charlottesville, VA: Hampton Roads, 2000.

Douglas Long   *Fundamentalists and Extremists.* New York: Facts On File, 2002.

Alf J. Mapp Jr.	*The Faiths of Our Fathers: What America's Founders Really Believed.* Lanham, MD: Rowman & Littlefield, 2003.
David Mills	*Atheist Universe: Why God Didn't Have a Thing to Do with It.* Philadelphia: Xlibris, 2004.
Michael Novak	*On Two Wings: Humble Faith and Common Sense at the American Founding.* San Francisco: Encounter Books, 2002.
Mark Oppenheimer	*Knocking on Heaven's Door: American Religion in the Age of Counterculture.* New Haven, CT: Yale University Press, 2003.
Sarah M. Pike	*New Age and Neopagan Religions in America.* New York: Columbia University Press, 2004.
Stephen R. Prothero	*American Jesus: How the Son of God Became a National Icon.* New York: Farrar, Straus and Giroux, 2003.
Marc Lee Raphael	*Judaism in America.* New York: Columbia University Press, 2003.
John Shelby Spong	*A New Christianity for a New World: Why Traditional Faith Is Dying and How a New Faith Is Being Born.* San Francisco: HarperSanFrancisco, 2002.
Stephen J. Stein	*Communities of Dissent: A History of Alternative Religions in America.* New York: Oxford University Press, 2003.
David A. Stout and Judith M. Buddenbaum, eds.	*Religion and Popular Culture: Studies on the Interaction of Worldviews.* Ames: Iowa State University Press, 2001.
Kenneth D. Wald	*Religion and Politics in the United States.* Lanham, MD: Rowman & Littlefield, 2003.
Jim Wallis	*Faith Works: Lessons from the Life of an Activist Preacher.* New York: Random House, 2000.
Clyde Wilcox	*Onward Christian Soldiers.* Boulder, CO: Westview, 2000.
Robert Wuthnow and John H. Evans, eds.	*The Quiet Hand of God: Faith-Based Activism and the Public Role of Mainline Protestantism.* Berkeley and Los Angeles: University of California Press, 2002.
Jonathan Zimmerman	*Whose America? Culture Wars in the Public Schools.* Cambridge, MA: Harvard University Press, 2002.

Index